DWIGHT MACDONALD ON
JAMES AGEE

"He had a positive genius for the wasteful and the self-destructive, always ready to sit up all night with anyone who happened to be around, or to go out at midnight looking for someone—talking passionately, brilliantly, but too much, reading aloud too much, making love too much, and in general cultivating the worst set of work habits in Greenwich Village. . . .

"When I heard of Jim Agee's death, the platitudes about "shock" and "loss" became real. I had always thought of Jim as the most broadly gifted American writer of my generation, the one who, if anybody pulled it off, might one day write a great book. . . ."

THE NEW YORK TIMES ON
JAMES AGEE'S LETTERS

"Comparable in importance to Fitzgerald's *The Crack-up* and Thomas Wolfe's letters as a self portrait of the artist in the modern scene."

THE LETTERS OF JAMES AGEE
TO FATHER FLYE

THE INTIMATE LETTERS OF A GREAT AMERICAN WRITER

Books by James Agee

LET US NOW PRAISE FAMOUS MEN
(with Walker Evans)

A DEATH IN THE FAMILY

AGEE ON FILM

Letters of
JAMES AGEE
to Father Flye

*This low-priced Bantam Book
has been completely reset in a type face
designed for easy reading, and was
printed from new plates. It contains the complete
text of the original hard-cover edition.*
NOT ONE WORD HAS BEEN OMITTED.

LETTERS OF JAMES AGEE TO FATHER FLYE

*A Bantam Book / published by arrangement with
George Braziller, Inc.*

PRINTING HISTORY

*Braziller edition published July 1962
2nd printing . . August 1962
3rd printing . . August 1962*

Book Find Club selection June 1962

Excerpts appeared in HARPER'S BAZAAR *July 1962*

Bantam edition published October 1963

CONTENTS

JAMES AGEE

A writer first and foremost—a born, sovereign prince of the English language—James Agee was also a prodigal and unself-preserving man, who imparted his extraordinary gifts to many forms, from verse to novels, film scripts to book reviews, friendship to marriage; who, at thirty-two, published a 450-page prose lyric called *Let Us Now Praise Famous Men* which is at the same time one of the most vulnerable perversities and surest glories of American literature; and who, at forty-five, died leaving a new novel on his desk, a film script in progress, committals as a man and a poet on every side, and as this first volume of his correspondence now makes clear, a thirty-year backlog of some of the most committed letters ever written.

By committed, I mean *inhabited*. In every one of these letters a human being is present: not just his beliefs and notions and moods, but something containing all these elements, that elusive essence of a complex personality which it usually takes a good novelist to purvey. Most writers leave letters, but only those of a fairly small number can be read, as Agee's can, by people not necessarily interested in the writer's other works. It seems to require a special gift in addition to the usual literary ones—the gift of being able to give oneself freely, or to cast one's bread on the waters. Some very eminent literary masters have lacked it. Keats had it, and in his own way, so did Henry James. But think of Joyce's letters—trivial and wooden; or Rilke's, or Gide's, so studied; or even Yeats', interesting but very cold. In even the most youthful of these letters of Agee, there is the warmth and rhythm of a living man, his tone, his pulse, the color of his soul, and probably the greatest gratification in reading them will come simply from making his acquaintance.

But there will be other rewards, too: the writing itself; the wide variety of felt experience; the wit; the acute literary judgments (I don't know a more just evaluation of Dreiser than the one rendered on page 25 when Agee was a ripe seventeen years old). In addition, these letters, as a unit, tell at least two stories about a man's life which I doubt if any other form— not even a film script or a novel by Agee himself— could have expressed so aptly. In fact, pondering these "stories" in their present epistolary form, I have even wondered why, when we look for masterpieces, we keep thinking in terms of novels and poems, when it may turn out that our truest, our subtlest uses of the word have gone underground and borrowed other, less official forms. Certainly this much seems to me to be true: nothing that Agee wrote in conventional forms—his verse, his *novella The Morning Watch*, his novel *A Death in the Family*—expresses his temperament any better, or more memorably than what he managed to do with his film column in *The Nation*, or a maverick commentary like *Let Us Now Praise Famous Men*, or such letters as those to be found in the present book.

Let me try to trace the first of the "stories," which for present purposes I shall call "Vocational Guidance." In the twenties and thirties, American writers and readers were teased by two myths, or prophecies, which still hovered in the air. One was the myth of the Great American Novel, that *sui generis* book which would reveal, or invent, the meaning of the

American experience once and for all. The other was the myth of the Promising Young Man, who would do with language what Lindbergh had done with flight—something bold and unprecedented and definitive, which would cross the Atlantic and speak for us to all the world. Fitzgerald and Hemingway and Wescott, among others, were setting the pace by 1930, but then, a few years later, Fitzgerald had confessed himself finished in *The Crack-Up*; Wescott appeared to have stopped writing; and Hemingway was giving more of his time to enacting the role in public than to fulfilling it in private.

Depression, bureaucracy, and political delusion all set in at once. The myth of the Great American Novel lapsed, and presently it got around that the Promising Young Man had mortgaged his birthright—had gone to Hollywood, or was writing for large-circulation magazines, or had learned to adapt his vision to the anonymous journalism being packaged several hundred feet above Rockefeller Plaza in the Time and Life Building. At the end of the last war, when *Let Us Now Praise Famous Men* was being remaindered in Manhattan bookshops,* and I myself first discovered Agee's name, he had already become a sort of scapegoat embodiment of this latter phase of the myth. Fugitive references to him always implied that he had been the best, absolutely, but that the best had somehow defected.

Yet as the course of these letters proclaims, no American writer, not even Henry James, ever had a more explicit, precocious, and God-fearing sense of a literary vocation. It is hard to be precise about just what this means, but covering pages with sentences is certainly at the heart of it; that, and a need (a need greater than any talent or luck or ambition) to use language to incarnate a part of oneself which no other

* The book was subsequently reissued by Houghton, Mifflin in 1960.

medium, including one's own flesh, will ever be adequate to. In varying degree, there is also the delight of playing the literary game, of making shapes with words, putting oblongs on squares, as Virginia Woolf has described it.

In all of these senses, James Agee had a marked vocation for literature. The earliest of these letters, written when he was not quite sixteen, mentions "a story and two or three poems" he is having published in the Exeter *Monthly*. In the very last letter, written a few days before his death, he speaks of taking the summer off to "finish my book." In between, over a period of thirty years, there is hardly a letter in which his calling is not mentioned or implied. And then listen to this, written in November, 1930, when he was twenty-one and still at Harvard:

> I don't know what I think of the poem itself but I'm from now on committed to writing with a horrible definiteness. . . . I'm thinking about it every minute. . . . I'd do anything on earth to become a really great writer. That's as sincere a thing as I've ever said. . . . I've got to strengthen those segments of my talent which are naturally weak; and must work out for myself a way of expressing what I want to write. You see, I should like to parallel, foolish as it sounds, what Shakespeare did. That is— in general—to write primarily about people, giving their emotions and dramas the expression that, because of its beauty and power, will be most likely to last. But—worse than that: I'd like, in a sense, to combine what Chekhov did with what Shakespeare did—that is, to move from the dim, rather eventless beauty of C. to huge geometric plots such as *Lear*.

It is a youthful letter—the aspiration strong and uncompromised as only youth's can be. But it is not frivolous. It is dead serious, and arises—vaults up—

out of a truly potent sense of destiny. How then did Agee do with his gifts what he did do? Why did he not write a dozen Chekhov-Shakespeare novels instead of a quarter of a million unsigned words for *Time* and *Fortune*?

Partly, of course, it was the time he lived in, "a low, dishonest decade," as Auden called it. When Agee came out of college in 1932, America was awash in a depression. As editor of the *Harvard Advocate*, he had devised an ingenious parody of *Time* magazine. It had caught the attention of the powers that be, and Agee was offered a trial job on *Fortune*. He accepted it—cub reporter, at $25.00 a week—and the consequences turned out to be complex and long-term. Indirectly, it may be said to have produced *Let Us Now Praise Famous Men*; it also channeled the better part of his energy into a decade and a half of anonymous prose.

But more than economics was involved. Another writer might have tried but given up, or been fired, lacking not only the discipline but the mobility of interest required for such a job. Agee was, by his very nature, able to bring a zestful and even inspired attention to almost anything or anyone. It was neither his strength nor his weakness. It was just the way he was. His capacity for taking an interest was legendary. There was no friend or passing acquaintance with whom he could not sit up all night, talking or listening with equal ardor. And what is most remarkable about his film criticism—in *Time* as well as *The Nation*—is its alertly searching, almost obstinate sympathy: it was a rare movie in which he could not find something to relish. This was not kindness. It was temperament. He was interested, always, and unlike most gifted men, not prudent, nor selective, nor limited. So, assigned to do a piece on orchids, or machine-made rugs, or Caribbean cruises, or the TVA, he would do it magnificently. But his own projects, dozens of them, had to wait; and the letters show it, along with his own suffering, year by year.

It is a poignant, harrowing story, true vocational guidance for poets to come, and as its protagonist Agee takes a place in America's mythology as well as its literature. It is odd, how we expect our best writers to do more than make us novels and poems. In Europe, works are all that is required of them, and they are honored accordingly. Here they must also use their bodies and personal histories and failures (above all, their failures) to make us *emblems*. And it is these emblems that we ultimately cherish. Is it for the truth in *Walden* that we still acknowledge Thoreau, or for the image of a superb Yankee crank that his own biography gives us? And didn't Poe, Melville, and Mark Twain, not to mention Hart Crane and Fitzgerald and most recently Hemingway, have to give us dramatic totems of themselves in order to make us take their work seriously? To these, and worthy of them, James Agee can now be added, with these letters as his testament, and the image of his scattered vocation as his didactic emblem.

The other "story" these letters have to tell is gentler, less intensive, but in a way even more moving, and entirely happy. Quite simply, it is about thirty-five years of friendship. When Rufus Agee—as he was called then—came to St. Andrew's School in 1919, he was just under ten years of age, and he had recently lost the father whom, much later, he described in *A Death in the Family*. Among the first persons he met was Father Flye, who himself had come to St. Andrew's only the year before, and who now lived with his wife in a cottage on the school grounds. Their household was busy, orderly, affectionate. There were plenty of books and Mrs. Flye painted portraits. In almost no time, Rufus had become a sort of foster son. It was with Father Flye

– 6 –

that he began to study French outside of school, and when he was sixteen, it was with Father Flye that he made his first and only trip to Europe. Between them, there developed the extraordinary quality of candor and trust which is reflected in the letters, and it is probably safe to say that each found in the other his lifetime's closest, most comprehensive friend.

Still, to the outsider, it is an unlikely combination. On the one hand, a quiet (though by no means quiescent) man of deep, vigorous faith, committed (though, again, not solemnly) to giving his life day by day to his vocation as a teacher. On the other, a passionate, exalted, yet in many ways intemperate and self-destructive young man, who passes from the relatively bucolic life of St. Andrew's, Exeter, and Harvard to become a New York intellectual, fully exposed to his generation's temptations, questionings and losses, and submerged in "destructive elements" of every kind—emotional, ideological, moral, aesthetic. In a dozen ways, these two men could not have been more different. Yet they had one thing in common, one abiding instinct, one area of response in which they were so alike that witnessing them together, I always thought of differing species belonging to the same genus. Perhaps the best instance of this alikeness that I can record here is a glimpse that I remember from an August night in 1953, a little less than two years before Agee's death. 1955

Father Flye had been in residence at St. Luke's Chapel on Hudson Street all that summer, conducting services and generally looking after the parish, and he had invited me to visit him there, to meet Agee for the first time. The weather was hot and humid, but we had plenty of ice cubes, as well as what goes best with them, and the basement kitchen was relatively cool. Agee, as always, was eloquent on a whole galaxy of subjects—Isherwood's novels; Marion Davies' emeralds, which, to his delight, she would wear to play tennis in; a certain scene, which he reconstructed frame by frame, from Dovchenko's *Frontier*; Chaplin's forthcoming *Limelight*; and his own Lincoln scripts, which were about to be filmed on location in Kentucky, and for a small role in which he was supposed to grow a beard. I listened, raptly, and Father Flye watched us both, eager, endorsing, alternately laughing and grave.

It was well after midnight before we remembered the time, and since Father Flye had an early mass in the morning, we went upstairs and began to bid him goodnight. But as we stood there in the hall, Agee spied the parlor piano, a bulkily carved, brownly gleaming upright, and moved over to pick out a tentative chord. Next he was seated, his large hands in ample possession of the keyboard, with the Episcopal Hymnal open before him. He began to play, Father Flye joined him, and a moment later they were singing together. For the first time, I think, I realized what it means when people are said to "raise their voices in song." Of course the hymns went back to their years together at St. Andrew's, but it was not nostalgia they were singing out of. It was an altogether hearty reverence, unsolemn and joyous, a reverence for everything, for the whole created world, and for all their differences, this was what they shared. In both of them, reverence was an inborn, inviolate instinct—neither a troubled conviction nor an act of faith, but simply an abounding, primary belief, as absolute as Blake's, that "everything that is, is holy."

Robert Phelps

INTRODUCTION

In the fall of 1918, I went to teach at St. Andrew's, a school for boys in Tennessee, about two miles from Sewanee, and continued as a member of the staff there for many years, my wife and I living in a house on the school grounds. The place was then, as it is now, under the direction of a monastic order in the Episcopal Church, the Order of the Holy Cross: a little school community in the country, on the Cumberland Plateau, having at that time some ninety pupils from the primary grades up through high school. Visitors and people from the neighborhood often came to Sunday services in the chapel; the religious tone was strong and pervasive, but of a friendly, natural and unaffected quality, far removed from anything of piosity or stuffiness.

Coming from Knoxville the next year, and taking a cottage for the summer at St. Andrew's, was a widow, Mrs. James Agee,* with her two children: James (or Rufus, as he was called then, using his middle name, which he afterward dropped), nine years old, and Emma, who was seven. At the end of the summer, with the cottage still available, Mrs. Agee decided to stay on through the winter and have the children attend the school. This arrangement continued for the next few years, with visits in the summers or holidays to the home of Mrs. Agee's parents in Knoxville

* Some people have had trouble with the pronunciation of this name. To get it right, say quickly the two letters A-G, with a strong accent on the A.

—the place which gave the setting for the sketch entitled "Knoxville: Summer 1915," used as the prelude to *A Death in the Family*.

Thus came about the friendship to which this book bears witness; beginning when the younger of the two friends was not quite ten years old, and continuing unchanged when he was forty-five, except by deepening and the maturity of years.

The relationship then, as later, was a happy, frank and sincere one of affection and respect on both sides, with the realization of a bond of understanding and the sharing in many basic feelings, instincts and sympathies such as can give the sense of real companionship in spirit. Age may not matter very much. I was a priest and a teacher, and in course of time he came to be in a class or two of mine, and there was an area of school relationship. But there could co-exist with this —and certainly not in Jim's case alone—a warm friendliness transcending the official. As an illustration of the quality of relationship I have in mind I might cite the instance when, having read an excellent final examination paper in history he had handed in (at the age of twelve), I found written at the end, "Goodbye till next year. — See you at lunch."

In the summer before he was sixteen, Jim and I spent several weeks in England and France, doing most of our traveling by bicycle. That fall he was to enter Phillips Exeter, in preparation for Harvard; and when we returned at the end of August, we parted in New York, I to return to St. Andrew's, and he to visit his mother, who had married again and was no longer living in Tennessee.

I realized that it would be some time before we met again, and as it turned out I saw him very little in the next eleven years. In May, 1936, he visited us at St. Andrew's, as mentioned in his letters. In the early 1940's, I began taking summer parish duty in New York (at St. Luke's Chapel in Greenwich Village).

This continued through 1954, and gave us many opportunities to meet and talk at length.

The letters which follow cover a period of just thirty years—from the time Jim entered Phillips Exeter to 1955, the year of his death. Some of these letters were typed, but most were in longhand. Those he sent from Exeter were written in ink, and fairly easy to read. Later, he used a well-sharpened pencil, and developed a very small handwriting which made reading a slow and at times a trying and well-nigh baffling task, but with rewards for the patient.

James Harold Flye

SPECIAL NOTE TO THIS EDITION

Some have felt they would be interested to read letters of mine to James Agee; but it seemed better not to divide the focus, and to have this his book alone, except for the inclusion of passages in italics from two verse letters of mine, one that was included in the first edition and the other that I had intended to include. Most of my correspondence with him, in fact, is not in existence, none before 1938 and with many wide gaps after that. It was not that he intentionally destroyed things he had written or collected, but with various circumstances of living and of moving, and conditions not conducive to order with writings and papers, much was at one time or another lost—his writings and other things—and that was the case with most of my letters to him.

LETTERS OF

JAMES AGEE

TO FATHER FLYE

Dear Fr. Flye:

I am terribly sorry not to have answered your letter sooner. I have been snowed under with work (I'm taking a schedule several times heavier than the average) and am only now shoveling out after two or three most harrowing weeks. Yes, it's more strenuous even than our sightseeing last summer . . . My grades will be coming in pretty soon, and whether they are good or bad, I'll send them to you—if you like.

All but one (or possibly two) of my teachers are very interesting. They stick to the curriculum only as much as they have to, and their ways of teaching are awfully interesting. I expected to see something of the modern methods of education you read about, but most of them are hardboiled and just a bit antagonistic towards students. My English work is most interesting of all, and the assignments foreshadow, in their gargantuan volume, four horrible years to come in college . . .

You may be interested: I know Freeman Lewis, Sinclair Lewis' nephew. He lives just down the street, and is very nice. He went with his uncle through slums in New York, getting material for the next book; it is very interesting. I have blown myself and bought *Arrowsmith* and a few books.

Have you read *Ariel,* a sort of fictionized biography of Shelley? It's lovely. Also *Elizabeth and her German Garden,* which I haven't read, but which is thought to be delightful. It's worth a try, I should think.

I have written stuff for the *Monthly,* and I am to

* Whenever the place or the date was omitted in Jim's original letter, I have put this information—insofar as I could determine it from postmarks—in brackets.

get a story and 2 or 3 poems in this month. This will get me into the Lantern Club, I hope. That is one of the big things to be in here. It runs the *Monthly*, and is a literary club. It gets several authors up each term who give very informal talks in the club room. Booth Tarkington, who graduated here, came several times, and Sinclair Lewis may come this winter. It's a swell idea to have such a thing in a school, don't you think?

I have just gotten Donn Byrne's *Blind Rafferty* from the very good library,—but I haven't had time yet to read it.

Dear love to you, Father, and to Mrs. Flye. I wish I could see you.

Rufus

[Exeter, New Hampshire]
Wednesday night.
[*March 3, 1926*]

Dear Fr. Flye:

I was so glad to get your letter . . .

There is an epidemic of scarlet fever here, and one of measles. Different sicknesses have ruined the whole term; everyone is miles behind in the work.

I'm going to spend my spring vacation in Cambridge with the Cowley Fathers. Frankly, I look forward to a dreary holiday. It's been a hard term and I feel like "cutting loose" rather than staying in a monastery. But it's a fine place to spend Holy Week —which is my vacation. I think it's pretty poor, even in a non-denominational school, to have the vacation then.

I'm sending a copy of the *Monthly* down. I have a play in, which is more or less the result of St. Andrew's.

A Mr. Warner, from Harvard, gave a tremendously interesting talk about his adventures in China. (He was trying to get sixth-century frescoes from some Buddhist cave-monasteries.) It was amazing. I didn't know such things happened outside Rider Haggard. It's very late, so I can't go on now. Suffice it to say that I was *much intrigued* by it all.

Love to Mrs. Flye too,

Rufus

[*Rockland, Maine*]
July 22, 1926

Dear Father Flye:

It's almost impossible and very discouraging to realize that my vacation is already a third over. I'm having a splendid summer here. But it can't compare with our trip last summer. I hope we can take another before very long.

Have you read *Mantrap,* Sinclair Lewis' latest book? It is so entirely different from the three others that I didn't know quite what to make of it. It seems like James Oliver Curwood backwoods drammer beautifully written. It shows an almost complete escape from satire, and a sort of freshness of plot that I'd never have expected of Lewis. (It also shows a good deal of slovenly writing.) I don't know the reason for the change, but I imagine from what his nephew says, that Lewis must have been almost sober during most of the time he wrote the book. It's always amusing, and towards the end it's really fine. And the characters are as real as Babbitt and Leora Tozer. So don't let the "trader, tenderfoot and a girl" wrappers scare you off it. I don't think it was intended as a potboiler; I have an idea it was written as a sort of relaxation from working on the biggest thing yet. That ought to be out before long.

And have you read anything by Rose Macaulay? *Orphan Island* is about as good a satire as you can get—a red-hot take-off on English Government in general and Queen Victoria in particular.—oh! it's juicy stuff.

I was lucky enough to get two prizes at Exeter—one was four volumes of Kipling, for furthering interest in Creative Writing, and the other was $30 for Composition. I managed to pass everything, including Latin, which is much more important.

I am trying to get hold of *Gentlemen Prefer Blondes*, which you recommended to me. You know Edith Wharton thinks it's the Great American Novel, whatever that means. *Beau Geste* is a rather good book—for adventure and mystery, especially.

I had hoped to go to Knoxville early in September, and if I had I was certainly coming up to see you at St. Andrew's. But the trip is very expensive, and my Grandmother and Uncle Hugh intend to live in New York this winter, so I must wait and see them at Christmas. I do hope some chance will come soon which will make it possible for us to see each other again.

Mother, and Fr. Wright* send their love.

Rufus

* Jim's stepfather.

Dear Father Flye:

I've been in Exeter exactly a month tonight. It seems like a year—or no time. I dreaded it horribly late in the summer—thought I'd never be able to get back to work again, but I have. In fact, I've worked more steadily than ever before. I think I'm practically sure of a scholarship, and possibly of honors. This morning I had a French test—a big one. I tried so desperately to make an A that I made a D+, my poorest mark yet. I was watching too carefully for the idiomatic contortions, and entirely overlooked some absolutely idiotic mistakes. I'm passing Latin now, but I'm not making a very good grade—I don't think. I made the surprising mark of 85 on the College Boards, so I'm supposed to be able to do better now.

Algebra is coming much easier than ever before. I've had three tests, and have made respectively 100, C, and 100. English is hard but most interesting—*Macbeth*. I'm taking Ancient History. They say the course under my teacher is better than the same in most colleges. My teacher is Dr. Chadwick, the head of the department. He has a rather imposing array of dates, time-parallels, and maps which are apparently silly—*but* besides he has a most delightful and lovely way of lecturing. Since I changed sections in the middle of the month, I was still behind on map work at the time of this test, so I was pretty inaccurate on that side of it, but he rated me very high and *magna cum complimentibus* in the argumentative or "splurge" questions. Nothing gives me more delight than getting hold of such a question that I've really read up on and "writing myself dry" on it.

One of the most "intriguing" of my courses is declamation, which isn't declamation at all, but elementary acting. The teacher seemed to me decidedly "ham" at first, but he's really a splendid man. He both writes and acts plays, and besides—or in spite of—that he is a scholar. He makes use of writhing, dope-fiendish gestures of his hands; he has a piano in his class-room, on which he splatters out vile chords; he leans against mantelpieces and sobs; and all the time he is enjoying the dumbbell's enjoyment of it.

Have you seen a book called *Nize Baby?* I think it's a really remarkable thing—certainly about the most original thing I've ever read. Have I sent you a play I wrote called *Catched?* A mountaineer play.

I had a summer that to almost anyone else would have been a bore. I happen to have been so prepared for it as to make it grand if harrowing. It was the vacation of what I suppose is a pretty typical High School Crowd. But the joke is that I'd never had such a summer before. I'd been in about the fix you were in; had perhaps two boy friends and not even an acquaintance among girls. But here, I had to swallow a dozen—or the dozen had to swallow me—hook line and sinker. All I did was to "run around" with this crowd. I learned to dance, after a fashion, and I've got over the worst, at any rate, of my bashfulness. I want to keep a certain amount of it; if there's anything that disgusts me, it's what's called "a smooth line." That's the main trouble with most of the kids—they're entirely insincere in everything they say.

But there was a surprising number of exceptions. There's one boy who's every bit as wide-read and intelligent as Oliver Hodge.* And another who was to room with me here but applied too late to get in at all. And a girl whom I fell violently for and loved forever—until I came away to Exeter. She's the most interesting egotist I ever ran into. But unalloyed egotism—or is it egoism—is wearing. I'm sorry; I doubt if she is. Finally, there's another girl who—well, I could and often do kick myself that I was so thick-

* A contemporary of Jim's at St. Andrew's.

skinned all summer. She's entirely devoid of the affected squawk and squeals and shiverings which ruin most girls—and the consequent vacuum is not filled by hot air, but by unobstreperous intelligence, tinged with a charming limeadish sarcasm.

Well, I'll cease to make a jackass of myself.

In the meantime it's a lot of fun to have somewhere to write besides home.

I hope that sometime you can manage to get up to Exeter. It's a beautiful town, and the school buildings are really fine. I had hoped to see you this Christmas, but Mother and Father plan to be in New York, so I guess I'll get no farther South than that. Someday I hope to get down to St. Andrew's again and see you and Mrs. Flye. Now we can write, anyway.

With love,
Rufus

[Exeter, New Hampshire]
[Dec. 14th, 1926]
Tuesday night

Dear Fr. Flye:

The term ends tomorrow morning, and I shall go straight to New York, where I shall be till after Christmas with my Grandmother and Uncle Hugh.

Later I'm going to visit in Rockland. Father, I do hope we'll see each other soon again. Occasionally I wake up with a jolt to the fact that I haven't seen you for over a year. And it's too bad that things are so fixed that it can't be helped. In getting these new friends and interests I don't forget you. But they pretty much absorb me, and I feel sorrier and sorrier that we can't be nearer together. I love you dearly, and I always shall.

That about Sam L—— is dreadfully sad.* It brings

* A good friend who had taken his own life.

me a little nearer realizing the difference between such a thing in fact and fiction. As I am now, I am able to read and write of the most sordid and sad things with rather impersonal interest; but as I come into actual contact with more and more gore, I have a more ghastly experience as a background for my literature. This is, of course, bromidic for an adult to hear, but it's quite new to me. I realize that before long I shall be quite as disgusted and horrified by realism as, say, Mother.

We gave the Christmas Play tonight—a cut *Taming of the Shrew*. I played Baptista, the wheezy old man. It went off quite well, and so did our director, immediately after the show. He went to New York; tomorrow sails for London.

Sometime I'm going to get together a lot of my writing and send it to you.

Love to you and Mrs. Flye,
Rufus

[*Exeter, New Hampshire*]
[*January 9, 1927*]

. . . I'm trying for one Essay Prize, offered by Viscount Bryce (I think). A frightful subject. "To what extent do the ramifications of International Trade affect the political relations of the U.S. and the British Empire?" The prize is a $500 round trip ticket to England and $500 more cash for expenses. Also letters to assorted diplomats. It would, I suppose, be very wonderful if I could win it. Somehow I don't greatly relish the idea of traveling alone, or in a prescribed group, and I'd have a ghastly time meeting diplomats. Besides, I'd be quite happy to go to Rockland again next summer. The best boy friend I have is there. And I'm very fond of a girl there. My—how I wish you knew both of them. I'd love to talk about them to you.

I plan to go with this friend on a three weeks' trip to Quebec, and roundabout through the French villages near it. We were there for a short time last year. . . .

Dear Father Flye:

I'm awfully sorry that you got the idea I'd won the National Prize. The newspapers got it wrong, and apparently the news spread. The thing I won is only the school prize; winning that made my essay eligible for the National Contest. If I win the *National* Contest I get the trip,—as it is, I get a small silver cup—some day. I certainly wish I could win it, but have little hope. For one thing, I really don't know much about the subject. But even then my chances are slight: for the past 2 years an Exeter boy has won, and I think the judges would feel in duty bound to give some other school the prize if at all possible. It's too bad all the congratulations have come for a thing I've never won. If I could win it, it would be wonderful. I understand they leave you to your own resources after a certain length of time; I don't know what I'd do, then. Go to France, probably . . .

Working on the essay has lowered my grades considerably, so that I'm in danger of losing my scholarship. Since the contest ended, though, I've been grinding. Only today we had a big test in history, which I imagine I got a good grade in, so I may pull through at that.

You used to tell me what to do—that is about relaxing my mind and body—when things tied up in knots. I didn't really know what you meant, but I do now. Rather often I get a horrible tight feeling as if I were wrapped in mummy-cloths. Sometimes I'm disgusted at myself, sometimes at the school or my friends—I was that way this evening—feeling inexplicably like crying or biting into something or beating it with my fists . . .

I've bought and read *Elmer Gantry*, the Lewis satire on religion. It's very disappointing, although excellent in spots. He's turning rancid.

Love,
Rufus

[*Exeter, New Hampshire*]
Wednesday night
April 20, 1927

Dear Father Flye:

I should have answered sooner, and am sorry to have failed to . . . I haven't your letter, but I think I can remember the principal things you said . . . I wish I could know the boy you wrote of. He sounds fine, and the thing you quoted is certainly good. Golly, what a relief it is to find here a whole crowd of really intelligent and cultured English teachers. There's a certain amount of routine, but most of the men are personally delightful, and spare no pains to give us large doses of their personalities. But the History courses are *lousy*. Everyone admits it. They're absolute and abject slaves of the College Board Requirements. This necessitates the squeezing out of all that is interesting in history. For instance, when we come to a chapter on realism in Hellenic sculpture, we skip it and go on to bigger and better things, such as the all-important fact that the battle of Zama was fought in 202, not in 203.

I've read very little until the past two weeks. In that time I've read *Manhattan Transfer*, by John Dos Passos. It's an unalleviatedly filthy book; when it's bellyfull of sexual filth it descends to coal-dust and orange-peels. But it's very cleverly done. I hate mere cleverness, so I'm glad to think there's more than that to it—he's really a marvelous writer, and the novel is built in an entirely new way. Also, I think for some reason that he writes filth sincerely disbelieving in the existence of anything else—that he's not a cheap hackwriter, writing Pay Dirt. And the book is full of lovely descriptions—passages of poetry as fine as any I know for color and beauty alone. Then I've read *The Plutocrat* by Tarkington. It's rather thin and tepid, but a delightful antidote for the more rabid and intolerant parts of Sinclair Lewis' books. The idea is to glorify Babbitt, to set him up as a barbaric giant Carthaginian—and at the same time to make rather small and foolish the people who belittle him. I thought Lewis had done it sufficiently in *Babbitt*; but this is much fairer. But by no means as great a book, since its very publication depends on the writing of *Babbitt*. I've today begun to read *An American Tragedy*, which seems rather fine, in spite of stormy criticism. Dreiser's English is bum, yet it has a peculiar beauty and excellence. You feel you're reading a rather inadequate translation of a very great foreign novel— Russian, probably. He's horribly obvious, and has no humor. But this dullness is a relief from the heady brilliance of Dos Passos or Lewis—and he has a tenderness, a love for his characters, that rarely slobbers and is usually strong and fine.

At the risk of repeating myself—I was elected Editor of the *Monthly* and President of the Lantern Club (the Literary Club). This last is going to be hard; I must make twittery, pleasant little introductory speeches, "To Exeter men, I am sure that Mr. Nathan needs no further introduction—Mr. Nathan."

During my spring vacation I was in Boston, and heard Beethoven's Mass, and the 6th, 7th, 8th, and 9th Symphonies. The 9th Symphony impressed me as nothing has ever before. I also saw Mrs. Fiske in *Ghosts*. It's immensely more harrowing on the stage. "Through pull" with an Irish Politician, I got to see the Morgue and the Jail, neither of which were what I'd expected, but rather worse, in a clammy, metallic way. I had a taste in my mouth as if I'd been licking an old sardine can.

I've heard nothing more from the Essay. For the School Prize I got a really pretty little gold cup, a watch charm. (I have no watch.)

I have one friend in school whom I care for as I do for you. Thinking of one of you automatically increases my fondness for the other. I don't know if you see what I mean; remembering you sort of gives a precedent to my feeling for him, and being his friend freshens my memory of you. I can't think that I could care for anything better than such a friendship. There seems to me at best so much possible in common between two people of the same sex—so much more to encourage friendship. A girl's brain is mysterious, but only in a superficial way—a way very exasperating to me. But this boy and you and I know how our thoughts work, what we are interested in and why—everything—no finessing, no nerve-twisting, egg-walking depreciation such as I feel you'd have even with a wife. I wish we could all three enjoy friendship together; I know you'd like each other.

Love,
Rufus

Dear Father Flye:

I was awfully glad to get your letter—and I'm sorry I hadn't written you. I had a perfectly frightful spring, beginning about when you wrote me last, and was too miserable to write anybody anything. My first inclination was to write you all about it, but I knew it would do neither of us any good—so I didn't write at all.

I haven't seen *Trader Horn*, but even from the reviews and ecstatic advertisements I saw, I gathered it was a rather lousy book. Every boy I know who has read it says the same thing. The woods seem to be full of literary hoaxes of one sort or another. One of them is a rather nice thing: *The Diary of a Young Lady of Fashion in the year 1765*—written in the year 1925 or so, by a nineteen year old Irish girl.

Did you read, in (I think) the July issue of the *Atlantic*, a prize-fighting story called *Fifty Grand?* The author, Ernest Hemingway, published a rather sensational novel, *The Sun Also Rises*, last year and this fall a book of short stories, *Men Without Women*. They're terrific, and fine—all I've read of them. Hemingway is one of the crowd of degenerate Americans who "settled"—if you could call their life a settling —in Paris, after the war. *Circus Parade*, by Jim Tully, is remarkable chiefly for its nakedness of style, and for uncovering the most abysmal brutality I've even imagined could exist. It's worth reading—if you think a thing of that sort would interest you.

I don't have such heavy work this year—for two years I've worked extra hard, to get a light schedule. I'm taking Chemistry, which is very hard for me but interesting. And I'm very fond of Ovid and Vergil. I've had a terrific time with Latin here, up to this year, but now I'm really enjoying it. There are one or two really great teachers of it here . . .

In French—which I have in a minute now—we're
reading *Quatre-vingt treize*. It's remarkable stuff—the
way Hugo stalls along, with superb but rather melo-
dramatic tricks to hold your interest—and his different tricks of exposition—it makes it interesting.

I must go.

Love,
Rufus

[*Exeter, New Hampshire*]
November 26, 1927

Dear Father Flye:

Thank you so much for the book.* I read a number
of his essays last summer in a book whose title I can't
remember. He writes very beautifully indeed. I particularly like his descriptions of natural scenery. You
know Grandpa thought *The Upton Letters* about the
nicest prose he knew, mother says.

I haven't seen you in such a long time. I wonder
when I shall again. Father I *know* we shall see each
other someday again, and not merely someday but
often. We're simply too dear to each other to go on,
just writing occasionally . . .

later

I've read the first of the Benson essays—"The Point
of View"—and I like it extremely, not only for the
mellowness and beauty of the writing but for what
he says, too. It's as thoroughly lovely a style as I
know of—and there must be a great number of men
who, like him, live quietly and beautifully, but who—
unlike him—never even write down their point of
view.

Do you know of *Lolly Willowes*, or *Mr. Fortune's
Maggot*, by Sylvia Townsend Warner? They're both

* I had sent him a copy of A. C. Benson's *From a College Window.*

quiet and unusual and beautiful books. I think you'd
be delighted with them—especially as you think of
them appearing in the midst of raucous splurges and
slops that is most fiction now. The same thing goes
for all of Robert Nathan's books. I'm going to read
his newest one soon. He writes with great simplicity
and *suggests* an infinite amount—and his work is as
much poetry as prose . . .

Love,
Rufus

[*Exeter, New Hampshire*]
[*December 31, 1927*]
Monday night

Dear Father:

I'm very much ashamed not to have answered
sooner. There's been school work, but that's always a
perennial and sickly excuse, and I don't want it to
count. All I want you to know is that it isn't that I
don't care anything about keeping you for a friend—
I'm just careless . . .

I've been reading *Leaves of Grass* since I came back.
You know, since last winter or so I've been feeling
something—a sort of universal—oh, I don't know,
feeling the beauty of everything, not excluding slop-
jars and foetuses—and a feeling of love for everything
—and now I've run into Walt Whitman—and it seems
as if I'd dived into a sort of infinitude of beautiful
stuff— all the better (for me) because it was just what
has been knocking at me unawares.

Recently I had to go into Boston to get fitted for
glasses. I have a slight astigmatism, nothing really
wrong. Dorothy went in, too, and we walked around
and ate and saw a play—*The Play's the Thing*, a very
suave little number that isn't worth two cents, but
was beautifully acted. We tried to get seats to *The*

Road to Rome. Heard of it? I kind of wish we'd seen it in New York, because while it doesn't claim to be serious history, it treats history from an angle I know you approve. That is, there is no attempt to get the Bulwer-Lytton type of sublime blah for soldiers—instead there's—Oh, an officer goes the length of a line of men, lined up for gladius inspection. Perfect silence till he comes to the end man to whom he bawls—"Hey. Ain't you been in the army long enough to know ya can't get away with a rusty gladius like that? What the hell you think this is?" And so on. With excretory jests about the guys back in the Elephant Brigade.

Then yesterday, I went down with another boy and some teachers and their wives to hear Rachmaninoff. The boy is good! He played three pieces which I heard Paderewski play this Christmas—and I grieve (genuine grief) to say there's no comparison.

Have you read *Sorrell and Son?* I haven't, but I saw (don't laugh) an excellent movie made of it. Filmed in England. Dorothy was with me, and (she's read it) says it follows the book word for word. So I do feel I've license to say it's a very beautiful and moving story—a real tragedy (in a way) with no dirty slush. And not overdone. Perhaps the best thing about it is that, while Sorrell had a terrible lot to stand, he had at least an equal number of lucky breaks. It's the most perfect thing on its theme that I can imagine. And its theme isn't to be sneezed at. I hope you'll read it if you haven't.

Love always,
Rufus

Dear Father Flye:

Apparently vacationing occupies more of my time than school—At any rate, this is the first vacant space I've had for writing.

I had some fear I wouldn't graduate—(at the end of the month before graduation I was flunking Plane Geometry and Chemistry)—I was laid up for a week with tonsilitis just at the end—a rather crucial time to get sick—but I pulled through after all.

I felt a good deal more deeply than I'd expected to about graduating. Not any of the threshold-of-life bellywash—(and they said amazingly little of that kind of stuff)—but simply that I'm fonder than I realized of Exeter, and know I'll never be nearly so much a part of the school again—not even if I give a couple of million for a baseball cage or a boiler plant.

I'm having a moderately dull time of it—not so much self-inflicted as usual, either. Dorothy is about 200 miles back in the White Mountains—and Brick Frohock—my best friend up here—sails tomorrow for France, for a year at the Sorbonne. So I'm left rather flat in that way. I'm reading a little bit—alternate chunks of Chaucer and of *The Great American Band-Wagon*, by that staunch Nordic Louie Marz—(Charles, I find his name is—but it should be Louie). It's loud-mouthed but amusing. I think M‒ ‒‒‒‒ Lewis roasted it fairly brown to begin with. Poor fool—he never will again. Apparently writing *Elmer Gantry* was too much for him—possibly he finds it necessary to "live" his characters . . .

I think it would be fun (if I get the power and friends) to try to revive the Harvard *Monthly*, which died of wounds rec'd in the Great War. It was far, far ahead of the *Advocate*, in every way. I've met a man who edited it, and through him heard of others who helped—and they're *not* at present, bond-salesmen. Conrad Aiken, E. E. Cummings, Heywood Broun (I think), Foster Damon, Robert Hillyer.

The man I met is S. Foster Damon, the recognized authority on William Blake, and America's authority on allegory and mysticism. He also writes beautiful verse, which sells high and seldom. One of the *Dial* mainstays—but better than you'd expect from such a report. (If I've written you this, skip it. I don't mean to repeat myself.) Brick gave him a copy of *Menalcas*, my Greek play, to read. (He's an English Prof. at Brown, Brick's college.) When I came down to see B. in the spring he heard (by chance) I was in town and invited us to supper. He told me he thought the poem was good and gave me some fifteen names and addresses to whom to send it for further criticism— Robert Frost, Edna St. Vincent Millay, Sara Teasdale, Robert Hillyer, Hilda Doolittle, Ezra Pound, etc. I saw R. Frost this spring; showed him *Pygmalion* and *Menalcas*—He said even better things of it than S. Foster —later another man, James Rorty, had a shot at *Menalcas*, and thought it good.—The general verdict is that I can do a lot if I don't give up and write advertisements. If I remain convinced they're right I'll croak before I write ads or sell bonds—or do anything except write. I've written another poem since then— rather long—around 500 lines—about a lady named Anne Garner. Of course a good deal of it is simply iambic prose—but I wrote that as a clothes-line on which to string my lyrics. It's funny—I can't write real lyrics—*subjective* things. I have to trump up a situation and story—and write them as of another character. I wish I could do it straight, as Housman does—Have you read *A Shropshire Lad* or *Last Poems*? they're perfect and lovely things—touch rock-bottom in disillusionment without a single line of cynicism, and without cheapness. And things so utterly simple.*

Don't you think that's beautiful stuff? (Probably you know it—even have the books in the house.)

No more time to write,

Love,
Rufus

[*Cambridge, Mass.*]
[*December 21, 1928*]
Friday: 1:30 A.M.

Dear Father Flye:

I started a letter to you just after receiving yours—and never finished it. I'm particularly sorry because it was reasonable to expect I'd be in New York this Christmas. I won't—I have to get my tonsils "scrapped," and won't even get a smell of New York. I'm awfully sorry not to see you, if you're going to be up.

Forgive the glib sound of this letter. It's the glibness of fatigue. Last week, being in the cast of the censored Dramatic Club play, I was up till 4 every morning—and I haven't yet caught up—what with work and an unofficial sort of insomnia.

I have read a good deal this fall, in the course of my studying—but little else except along the lines of witchcraft, demonology, etc. There's a magnificent library of that stuff here—real source material, a lot of it.

Tonight, with the Germanic Museum as a setting (3 lovely German Cathedral doors) the D. Club gave a Miracle Play from the Dublin Cycle—which, because of rotten luck (being dragged out to a lousy vaudeville) I missed.

* At this point Jim quoted "Far, far from eve and morning," "When I was one-and-twenty," "Is my team ploughing?", "If it chance your eye offend you," and "As I gird on for fighting," in full.

I've written little and poorly for the most part—chiefly for the *Lampoon.*

My studies are generally interesting except that my English is a sort of Cook's Tour of English Literature very smugly presented. I'm taking Geology (not as interesting as at St. Andrew's), Horace-Plautus-Terence—quite swell—European History—(wonderfully lectured)—and the English. My grades are fair—B in Latin—C in the rest.

I have drunk little and—I am glad to say—not yet to the point of saturation. I am drinking, as I write, a fearful and wonderful mixture of de-alcoholized Benedictine and—to give it taste—gin. The result rather strongly (very powerfully) resembles real Benedictine.

Have you read *The Time of Man* by Elizabeth Madox Roberts? I had hoped to give it to you for Christmas, but came across the Leonardo book which I understand is very fine—so gave that. The *Time* book's lovely.

Vacation begins tomorrow. I've not given it a thought, strangely enough—very different from my feeling at Exeter.

I go rather often to St. Francis' House—they're a fine bunch of men there. None of them I've seen have fallen into any of the familiar monastic eccentricities.

I wish I could write a decent letter but I'm almost in a state of coma.

My love to you and to Mrs. Flye,

Rufus

Dear Father Flye:

It's been a long time since I wrote you and so much uneventful has happened since then I can probably remember nothing worth writing, except that a fog in which I've been for months seems to be partially lifting—in other words I may, for one thing, be on the verge of writing some more. I've done very little since last spring. I've felt (for a while) rather petrified mentally and spiritually, and what few gratifying times I've got loose from it have produced nothing in the way of writing—which is a shallow criterion, I know, yet one which means a good deal to me. One trouble with my failure to write more is, I've been too ambitious. Last spring I was lucky enough to write something which more or less gave me a chance to say everything I had to say or feel about nature and death and a few such things. So, ever since, when I've really wanted to write—I've been unable to, because anything I could think of seemed so far below that in standard and opportunity. It wasn't conceit at all—a good deal more like desperation. Now I'm catching on to that, and am ready to welcome and do what I can with any idea that would seem to make a fair story or poem.

My writing this fall and winter has been restricted to one short story—generally considered horribly filthy—(It isn't exactly a pretty one, I'll admit)—and about a dozen short poems, most of them light—and half a dozen translations of odes of Horace. That's the most fun, because the easiest to do—in a way. The other day I started to work translating a poem of Housman's, written in Latin. It's a fine thing in Latin, and I doubt I can ever get it to sound like Housman's English. However, considering how I worship him, it's worth trying.

I've been reading a good deal of John Donne and Herbert, Vaughan, and Emily Dickinson, whose work bears a remarkable resemblance to Donne. Have you seen Jolas' Anthology of American Verse? One poem of almost every American poet—translated into French. Some of the translations seem good, but *The Congo*, which shouldn't even have been tried, is laughable.

Did you know of the Fifth Book of Horace? It was written by an eminent Oxford scholar, with translations by Kipling and Graves, and perfectly swell mock-pedantic notes by the author.

I've finally decided to major in Latin and English— am quite squeamish about the latter, so guess I'll do most consistent work in Latin and Medieval Latin, with (I hope) excursions into Egyptology, Chinese Civilization, Greek Archaeology, French, and Comparative Literature. Next year I'm taking Elementary Greek (terribly hard here); "Rousseau and his Influence," given by Babbitt, a most bitter classicist; "The Historical and Intellectual Background of English Literature"—not so good as it sounds—and in Latin a half course on the philosophers Cicero and Lucretius, and another on Horace, Martial, Juvenal . . .

I hope things so work out that I can see you again this summer. My love to you and Mrs. Flye,

Rufus

Dear Father Flye:

When I got home, Sept. 8th, I found your letter waiting. It had been balled up in forwarding. Sat down and half-answered it, but as usual with everything, never finished it.

I had a good summer: hard work and little time or provocation to be unhappy. I'd hoped it would effect a reasonably permanent cure for the irrational side of my unhappiness, but no such luck. I'm just about where I started. On the whole this year bids fair to be better in some ways: courses, friends, schedule—and bad enough in others to balance it up.

I feel more and more a growth of mental balance and appreciation, and it hits me, I suppose, about as puberty did. I experience the same almost sensuous joy in knowing that I'm "getting somewhere"—growing up. At exactly the same time, I'm conscious of a gradual spiritual and ethical atrophy. This I feel not so much in connection with religion and general morality as in my unconscious attitude, and in the reactions of old friends. It isn't in any respect a feeling of snobbery or superiority: for one thing I know many of them are a long way ahead of me. Nor is it that I'm affecting any new manner or attitude. I feel most sympathetic and understanding. Yet I feel as if my mind were turning into a wart, and that I can do nothing to stop it.

Even so, I have an idea it'll turn out all right. So long as I don't ignore this worry, etc., I'm not wholly lost. I suppose this is a perfectly natural phase of intellectual development—just as a flood of unpleasantly dirty thoughts and desires are a natural part of puberty. I'll outgrow this mess, then, as I've outgrown (to a great extent) the dirtier of my pubescent imaginings. At the same time, it's painful to feel as helpless about it as I do.

I was awfully glad to see Frank Smith—and very sorry that because of final exams I couldn't see him more. I talked to him some about Exeter, and he liked the idea. But we hadn't time to go much further than talking about it. What do you think of it? Exeter can be inexpensive for a fellow as intelligent as I feel he is —and it's the finest school I know. I think he'd benefit greatly—as almost anybody would—by a year or so in such a place. If you like the idea, let me know, and I can easily make the necessary overtures . . .

I've read very little in the past year. A few books on witchcraft, a good deal (comparatively speaking) of Latin, and a few novels, nearly complete the list. Just now am reading a remarkable novel, *The Innocent Voyage,* by Richard Hughes. I'm enclosing a review of it by a friend of mine, which gives you a better idea of it than I could. I think it would interest you—as *The Gypsy* by W. B. Trites certainly would. It's about the finest modern novel I know. It's at least in the class with *Ethan Frome,* if not above it. For perfection of style I know few things like it. It's written with most admirable economy of description and incident. And it deals about as ultimate a blow to the stream-of-consciousness type of writing as I could hope to see. Every thought is clear, yet very few are expressed, or even obviously suggested. It's as direct as the best passages I know in the Bible.

I'm reading Catullus now—and that's about all the Latin I *am* reading. He's certainly more pleasant than Horace, though I wouldn't call him as fine a poet; or, on the whole, so easy to translate into conventional lyrics.

I'm taking the following courses:

Lake's *Old Testament:*
From all I can gather, very amusing, very interesting, and very Unitarian.

English Literature—1603 to the Restoration:
> Should be a splendid course. It's an awfully diverse and complex period, and, with the sort of teaching it has, gives a great chance for original work—if I'm capable of doing it.

Philosophy B:
> An introductory course, attacking thus the study of the *types* of Philosophy.

Latin I:
> Catullus, Pliny, Tacitus, Martial.

Am drinking some; am not particularly fond of it. Gin, Rye, Scotch, etc. comprise the only commonly accessible drinks; and I prefer wine . . .

On the whole, an occasional alcoholic bender satisfies me fairly well. Don't, please, get the idea that this invariably ends in drunkenness. That seldom happens unless I'm down in the dumps at the time . . .

Are you to come north Christmas vacation? I hope so; I believe I'll be in New York, and so can see you.

Love to you and Mrs. Flye,

Rufus

November 19th, 1930

Dear Father Flye:

Last summer, and more this fall, I've thought of you often, and wished I could see you, and intended to write you. Until now I haven't even begun and lost a letter to you—as I did several times last spring. I'd like to make this a long letter, and a good one; but as is usual these days I feel fairly tongue-tied the minute I have a sheet of paper before me. If I could see you for any decent length of time, I'd without effort say what here I can't write. But I haven't seen you or even written you in a very long time—and would like if possible to give some sort of account of myself in the interim. That's a difficult job for me, and I don't know just how to go about it.

I suppose the two chief things that have happened to me, and that after a fashion include the others, have to do with what I want to do with my life, and with the nasty process of growing up, or developing, or whatever it may best be called.

So far as I can tell, I definitely want to write—probably poetry in the main. At any rate, nothing else holds me in the same way. As you know, I had two other interests just as strong a few years ago—music and directing movies of my own authorship. These have slowly been killed off, partly by brute and voluntary force on my part, chiefly by the overcrowding of my wish to write. Each of them occasionally flares up; last spring I was all but ready to quit college and bum to California and trust to luck for the rest. And more often, I feel I'd give anything to have forgotten everything but music, because I want so to compose. I really think I could have done it—possibly better than writing. I suppose a native inertia has as much to do with my keeping on with writing instead, as has an instinct (which I over-credit) for knowing that writing is my one even moderate talent.

Up to 6 or 8 months ago, I took this with onl\
radic seriousness. But as I read more and wrote \
what more carefully, it took hold of me more.\
spring I finished a fairly longish poem that fir\
finished the business. For one thing, I worked ha\
on it than ever before. And, when it was finished, \
ious people thought it was very good, and encourag\
me a good deal. I don't know what I think of the poe\
itself—but I'm from now on committed to writin\
with a horrible definiteness.

In fact it amounts to a rather unhealthy obsession.
I'm thinking about it every waking minute, in one way
or another; and my head is spinning and often—as
now—dull with the continuous overwork. The sad
part of it—but necessary—is that, most of the time,
I'm absorbed in no tangible subject that can be
thought through and put aside. The thing I'm trying
hardest to do is, to decide what I want to write, and
in exactly what way. After a fashion, I know, but it
will take a lot more time before I'm able to do it. The
great trouble is, I'm terribly anxious to do as well
as I possibly can. It sounds conceited; whether it is or
not: I'd do anything on earth to become a really great
writer. That's as sincere a thing as I've every said. Do
you see, though, where it leads me? In the first place
I have no faith to speak of in my native ability to become more than a very minor writer. My intellectual
pelvic girdle simply is not Miltonically wide. So, I
have, pretty much, to keep same on stretcher, or more
properly a rack, day and night. I've got to make my
mind as broad and deep and rich as possible, as quick
and fluent as possible; abnormally sympathetic and
yet perfectly balanced. At the same time, I've got to
strengthen those segments of my talent which are
naturally weak; and must work out for myself a way
of expressing what I want to write. You see, I should
like to parallel, foolish as it sounds, what Shakespeare
did. That is, in general—to write primarily about

-giving their emotions and dramas the expres-
t, because of its beauty and power, will be
ly to last. But—worse than that: I'd like, in a
o combine what Chekhov did with what
eare did—that is, to move from the dim, ra-
ntless beauty of C. to huge geometric plots
Lear. And to make this transition without its
ridiculous. And to do the whole so that it
aturally, and yet, so that the whole—words,
, characters, situation, etc.—has a discernible
try and a very definite *musical* quality—inac-
ly speaking—I want to *write symphonies*. That
character introduced quietly (as are themes in a
mphony, say) will recur in new lights, with new
erbal orchestration, will work into counterpoint and
get a sort of monstrous grinding beauty—and so on.
By now you probably see what I mean at least as well
as I do.

Well—this can't be done to best advantage in a
novel. Prose holds you down from the possibility of
such music. And put into poetic drama, it would certainly be stillborn or worse; besides, much of what I
want to get can't well be expressed in dialogue. It's
got to be narrative poetry, but of a sort that so far as
I know has never been tried. In the sort I've read,
the medium is too stiff to allow you to get exactly a
finely shaded atmosphere, for instance—in brief, to
get the effects that *can* be got in a short story or novel.
I've thought of inventing a sort of amphibious style—
prose that would run into poetry when the occasion
demanded poetic expression. That may be the solution; but I don't entirely like the idea. What I want to
do is, to devise a poetic diction that will cover the
whole range of events as perfectly and evenly as skin
covers every organ, vital as well as trivial, of the human body. And this style can't, of course, be incongruous, no matter what I'm writing about. For
instance, I'm quite determined to include comedy in

it—of a sort that would demand realistic slangy dialogue and description.

That leads to another thing—the use of words in general. I'm very anxious not to fall into archaism or "literary" diction. I want my vocabulary to have a very large range, but the words *must* be alive.

Well, that's one thing that keeps me busy: you can see what it leads to. For instance, what sort of characters to use? I want them to be of the present day—at least superficially. Well, present-day characters are obviously good for novels, but not so obviously material for high poetry. Further, just how shall they speak? At the climaxes they certainly can't speak realistically: and in the calmer stretches it would be just as silly for them to speak idealized blank verse.

Life is too short to try to go further into details about this. But it's part of what serves to keep me busy; and unhappy. The whole thing still seems just within the bounds of possible achievement; but highly improbable. There are too many other things crowding in to ruin it: the whole course of everyday life. And yet, of course, it's absolutely necessary for me to live as easily and calmly and fully as I can; and to be and feel human rather than coldblooded about the whole thing. It's only too easy, I find, to be "Human." I care as much as I ever did about other people's feelings, and worry much more when I hurt them. Of course I should be and am thankful for this, but it certainly helps complicate matters. For one thing, with most of my best friends, I feel rather dumb. I don't like to be unhappy or introspective to any noticeable extent in their presence; the result is that I'm pretty dull. Also, most of them are graduated or otherwise removed from the neighborhood, so that I'm pretty awfully lonely a good deal of the time. I'm too preoccupied with the whole business sketched in above to give my courses constant or thorough attention; I don't do much actual work; yet I feel exhausted most of the time. There are a few ways of relaxing, to a certain extent; I like to walk—especially at night; but frequently am too tired. I love to listen to music; but that involves being parasitic around music stores, or cutting classes to get rush seat at Friday symphony. At times, I like to play the piano. Just now, I'm cracked about it, having got a lovely thing by Cesar Franck: Prelude, Fugue and Variation. I played it for three hours tonight. I've been to half-a-dozen movies, one play, and three concerts. Once a week or so Franklin Miner comes in from the suburbs and we take a walk and eat together. I see a young tutor named Ted Spencer when I can . . .

I've got to stop, and get to bed soon. This isn't as full a letter as I'd like to have written, but I'm deadly tired. I hope you'll write soon—and I shall, too. Will you tell me about any further plans for your school? And about yourself and Mrs. Flye? I wish I could see you both again. Are you by any chance coming north this Christmas? Maybe I could see you then. I hope you are.

Much love to you both,

Rufus.

Dear Father Flye:

Before I write you I'd like to read all of your article*
(of which I've read part), but I'm too anxious to write
you. Seeing that, and hearing that you are to be in
New York during the next few days, plus the fact that
it is Christmas, has made me think a great deal about
you during the past few days I've been home. There's
such a great deal I'd like to write you, which would
require such involved and straying prefaces and ex-
planations—all of this, I'd give a great deal to see you,
and talk of for days and weeks on end. Not that, in
themselves, any of them are very important⸴ but all
are the things I wish I could tell of myself and ask of·
you—and probably shan't, because I boggle things
pretty badly in letters—I limp consistently, and move
in from concentrics around whatever unsteady subject
I'm trying to get at.

The trouble is, of course, that I'd like to write you a
pretty indefinitely long letter, and talk about everything under the sun we *would* talk about, if we could
see each other. And we'd probably talk five or six
hundred pages—so, as usual when I write you, it's so
difficult to select a few things from the five hundred
pages I'd like to write that I'll probably (again as
usual) give you a very fragmentary and generally un-
satisfactory idea of what I want to say . . .

A year ago makes a fair beginning: A year ago I
was in the same house, reading a little, playing the piano a good deal, playing the Brahms First (birthday
gift from mother and father) on the phonograph, and
writing what I could, which wasn't much.

I think I've told you of the Saunders, but I'm not
sure. I first met them a year ago last spring, through
Ted Spencer (who has helped me a great deal at

---

* "Some Movements in Modern Education," published in *The Sewanee
Review*, January 1932.

Harvard), and got to know them within the next week by applying through them for a teaching job. They advised me rather to finish college: I did, and am glad. As for them—I wish you could know them, as I wish all my friends could know you, and vice versa—but more than any, that the Saunders knew you. Inevitably barring one's own family, they're the most beautiful and most happy to know and watch, I've ever seen. It's hard to write of such people without becoming mawkish. I shouldn't—and probably shan't, much. Mr. Saunders is something like my grandfather, with the bitterness and unhappiness removed, but with the same calm, beauty and fortitude. I don't know how brilliant a man he might have been, if he'd grimly fought out one of his talents (music most likely, or painting): at any rate, he evidently decided, when he was quite young, not to try it: rather, to work calmly and hard, but with no egoism, on *all* the things he cared most about—and he's resolved his life into the most complete and genuine happiness I know. He has the perfect balance between intro- and extraversion, the Greek *moderation*—and about everything, except religion. His wife is exactly opposite in every respect of nervous and mental make-up—and in her high-strung and intense, electric way, as perfectly balanced as he. They have two daughters, respectively like their father and mother, and a son who would now be 25, and who died at fifteen, and whose letters and poems I have read: very lovely things: I believe as they do, that he had great promise: and can see that as a person he was one in a thousand; and another son, now 19; and like all the others fine and lovable.

I'm sorry for this digression and tabulation: it's just the sort of thing I meant when I said there's so much to *say* which can't adequately or even decently be written. An awful lot must be boring in letters (and therefore better left out) which in conversation would be absorbing—for a dozen obvious reasons.

Well, at any rate, I was lucky enough to be liked by them, and to have them now almost as near me as my own family: and, a year ago, was looking forward to the winter the younger of the daughters and a friend of hers whom I had come to know, would spend in Cambridge . . . They came in January and stayed out the term, taking courses, studying music, and seeing friends . . . Aside from them, the friend I saw most that year was Franklin Miner: crazy about archaeology, languages (knows 14), national characteristics, the theatre, and German literature, (more or less in order). I saw him a great deal.

But altogether the most important thing in that spring was I. A. Richards, a visiting professor from Cambridge. It's perfectly impossible for me to define anything about him or about what he taught—but it was a matter of getting frequent and infinite vistas of perfection in beauty, strength, symmetry, greatness— and the reasons for them, in poetry and in living. He's a sort of fusion of Hamlet and some Dostoevsky character, with their frustration of madness cleared away, and a perfect centre left that understands evil and death and pain, and values them, without torment or perplexity. This sounds extravagant—well, his power over people was extravagant, and almost unlimited. Everyone who knew him was left in a clear, tingling daze, at the beginning of the summer. It stayed, and grew, all summer.

I spent the summer at home, reading and writing. Though little of it is really finished, I got a good deal down on paper—about 600 lines of poetry and about 20,000 words of prose—and a lot of reading—chiefly Dostoevsky's *The Possessed*, which simply set fire to all that Richards planted for it. It was a very quiet summer, alternating almost by weeks an exalted with a completely ruined feeling. But, much more than I realized, these things Richards had done were fermenting.

The last three weeks before school I spent at the Saunders. I. A. Richards was there part of the time, and that wasn't without its effect. (He, by the way, thinks my poetry good—maybe more than good.) The main thing there was coming closer to all of them and really knowing their son for the first time, and getting to know Via and talk with her as I never had before . . . There again Richards and (inadvertently) Dostoevsky were responsible. We began to sit up all night, talking without any limit of time or subject. Via and her friend were coming back to Cambridge for the year; I was glad of that. I was very much moved and excited by these new friendships . . .

So— I came back to Cambridge, lowing at the skies, all my silken flanks with garlands drest, stridently happy and energetic and writhing with schemes of regularity and moderation and with eagerness for the year to begin. It began, Bang . . . I was frantically reading for and taking exams which count 30% of four years work. Regularity began, and moderation ceased. So, with a few let-downs, it has been, ever since. The regularity has been this: an average of 3½ hours sleep per night; 2 or 3 meals per day. Rest of the time: work, or time spent with friends. About 3 nights a week I've talked all night, usually with Via or Upham. The work has been variegated and often without result and usually without system. Pretty consistently, I've worked till 5 every day: at the magazine, courses, reading, my own writing, tutorial reading. Then, pretty consistently, I've seen friends: and this has been so peculiarly intense that it might well be called work: it has, at any rate, been at least as exhausting as any work I've ever done. It's the most extraordinary and grand 3 months of my life—and I think has been so for many other people. The reasons are easy to think of but hard to put down: everything going *continuously* at top speed—mind, body and nerves; and with an intensity I've never known before: with powers, pain and joy all humming at once; with everything at once terrifically actual, yet abstracted and clear as glass: even dull and microscopic things seemed magnificently alive and exciting: and very little was dull and microscopic . . .

Well, this reduced more and more to a purely emotional account: far from what I'd expected. My study and reading and writing has been so broken across it that I can't collect any sort of record of it. A good deal of Wordsworth and Donne and Joyce, and some Chaucer, and Coleridge, are the main things, with emphasis all on Wordsworth, Joyce and music. What writing I've done has been done almost rigidly as if I were composing music—not in accordance to definite musical form, but in intricacy of structure, recurrence of themes, and an attempt to write *impersonally* —the difference between pure music and program music . . .

I'm in process of applying for a fellowship to Oxford or Cambridge, and am hunting for teaching jobs. Also, more immediately, and taking much more time, I'm engineering a parody of *Time*, to be published by my magazine—and must do as much as possible on it before vacation is over—when I must start work on exams. So—I'll have to get to work now. If I had the money, I'd be seeing you in New York these days— but I am next door to penniless, except for college bills.

My love to Mrs. Flye and to you—and all my wishes that this year will see your school started.

Rufus.

Dear Father Flye:

I'd thought I could write a long letter today—but got involved, all afternoon and evening, in trying to write poetry. I wrote myself into a bad headache and am now too stupid for much of anything. For the past two weeks, particularly, writing has been very much on my mind. I've been steadily trying to do it, and haven't written a single good thing. The only writing I do which approaches decency is on this job—and on other stuff I seem to be pretty well congealed. For one thing I'm emotionally stupefied, and have very little and dull and unextensive imagination.

One thing I feel is this: that a great deal of poetry is the product of adolescence—or of an emotionally adolescent frame of mind: and that as this state of mind changes, poetry is likely to dry up. I think most people let it; and that the one chance is to keep fighting and trying as hard as possible. That doesn't hold water—nothing I think does now. But it seems somewhat better to *try* than to quit the job entirely.

Father, I can't tell you what I mean about this or anything else. I've been used to bad spells of despondency always, but this is something else again; it seems to be a rapid settling into despair of everything I want and everything about myself. If I am, as I seem to be, dying on my feet mentally and spiritually, and can do nothing about it, I'd prefer not to know I was dying . . . I've felt like suicide for weeks now—and not just fooling with the idea, but feeling seriously on the edge of it . . . I know I should be able to fight my way out of this, and I hate and fear suicide, but I don't have a thought that isn't pain and despair of one sort or another. Knowing how rotten the thoughts are, instead of making them better makes the whole thing worse. I simply am not capable of being the kind of person, doing the kinds of things, which I want to be. And I haven't enough good in me to realize the filthiness of this discontent, and to reconcile myself to it. I would certainly prefer death to reconciling myself.

Mother writes that you're reading the Chekhov stories. There's another volume there somewhere around—it would be worth hunting. I don't like many things as well. Have you read his plays? I remember that we saw *The Cherry Orchard* in London. I've seen it several times since; and read it aloud several times. I wish we could read those plays aloud now.

And certainly I wish I could see you and talk to you. But one of the damnable things about me now is that when I write or speak to anyone I love, I become so fouled in my own rottenness that I can write nothing else.

God bless you and help me.

Rufus

Better today—Monday night.

Dear Father:

Thank you—I can't tell you how much—for your letter. First of all let me tell you I'm a lot better—and I think pretty well out of the area of suicidal thought. I can promise you that I was never delighted with the idea—and knew how perversely I was inclined to it. The thing I dreaded was—what I came near—doing it almost mechanically, without thought. I expect it's most frequently done that way—provoked finally by some reason which, even as you act, you know is a microscopic one. The vicious thing which brings you nearest it (and which, if a grain of the mind were positive would drive you from it to fight) is self-hatred, so fas as I'm concerned. So that the most cruel things about it—which of course you realize at the time—condense and reinforce your self-contempt. But all this is merely talk—because as I say, I'm out of it now, and I think am going to be thoroughly well very soon. If I am, I should have no reason to fear anything of that sort for a long time to come.

The *epidemic* of despair and weariness you speak of is a terrible thing. The whole spiritual *tone* of this time seems the darkest and saddest in centuries. I hardly know which it seems worse in—women or men. Very pitiable—and very different—in both. Lately the aspects that bring women down have involved me much more immediately. I hardly know a one of any vulnerability and beauty of spirit who isn't at least touched by it—above all, women under about thirty. Along with all the great good it has done in that direction, science and scientific-quasi-ethical thought has brought something almost like destruction into love. To say nothing of the *foul* results of *feminism*. It may resolve for the women of the next generation or two but this generation suffers hell for it: trying to live an uneasy egocentricity they can't sustain, unable to reconcile it with love, which they could, and ruined in love by the grinding of old conventions to which they've been trained, against new conventions which they honestly feel compelled to live by: wanting marriage and avoiding it—and many times so hurt and dulled by the fractures and foulnesses of the love they experience that they lose all capacity for the sort they've always wanted. I know three painfully caught in some such situation now, and a younger fourth who is probably headed for worse . . .

Father, I wish most of all I could have been nearer you through the past few years, and I hope deeply I can from the near future on. I'm poor at writing letters. Even if I weren't, correspondences are pretty bleak, compared to actual seeing. I feel that so much about you and about my uncle Hugh—that there is something sad and crazy about passing year after year of fairly short life in such poor communication with people you care for. It gives you even a sense of sorrow in the new friends you make—for the closeness of any friendship can't help including in thought all the people with whom you've known the same thing. And that has a lot to do with the sadness—that all those people don't know each other—and the larger sadness (against all *reason*) when any two of them fail to like each other as well. When you have a sense of the best in your friendship, you feel without vanity but very clearly, the establishment of a sort of common spirit, almost an Olympian sort of thing, that is much finer than any one person in it—and you feel that the thing concerted and fully and mutually realized by even a few dozen people, could not fail to make a better thing of the world.

Are you fond of Swift? I never read him till last winter, and am re-reading *Gulliver's Travels* now. I can't *say* the love and dumb reverence for him I feel.

I don't think many people have ever lived with as little compromise to the cruelties in human nature, with such acute pain at the sight of them, and such profound love for what the human race *could or might be*. People who call him a Hater of Humanity make me writhe—they are likely to be the very hardest of all human sorts to show true humanity to—because they *are* by intention kind and easy-living, and *resigned* to the expedient corruption of living quietly and happily in the world.

When you get down here again I'll have my phonograph working—not here but in my office, to play at night. An empty skyscraper is just about an ideal place for it—with the volume it has. Something attracts me very much about playing Beethoven's Ninth Symphony there—with all New York about 600 feet below you, and with that *swell* ode, taking in the whole earth, and with everyone on earth supposedly singing it; all that estranged them and all except joy and the whole common world-love and brotherhood idea forgotten. With Joy speaking over them: O ye millions, I embrace you . . . I kiss all the world . . . and all mankind shall be as brothers beneath thy tender and wide wings.

In all this depression over the world, and the whole Communist thing, I get two such feelings as strongly as I have the capacity for them: one the feeling of that music—of a love and pity and joy that nearly floors you, and the other of Swift's sort, when you see the people you love—any mob of them in this block I live in—with a tincture of sickness and cruelty and selfishness in the faces of most of them, sometimes an apparently total and universal *blindness* to kindliness and good and beauty. You have a feeling that they could never be cured and that all effort is misspent— and then you also know the generations of training in pain that have made the evil in them, and know it would be more than worth dying for.

I look forward to seeing you when you come down. And I hope you can conveniently stay at least a few days. It will be very easy and inexpensive here.

Rufus

[New York City]
[October 25, 1932]
Tuesday

Dear Father Flye:

I've been wanting the sense of time, and lacking it, for weeks, to write you a letter—because I don't like to write notes. All the same, this will be a note, because I have no time I can rightly call my own just now. The thing that made me nevertheless take a jump at the typewriter was noticing in the *New Republic* that a gentleman named Cuthbert Wright is teaching this year at St. Andrew's. Last year (and I guess for years before that, off and on) he was at Harvard. I never knew him. A friend of mine, Talbot Donaldson, did. He used to send in many things to the *Advocate*. I'm very curious to know whether you know him well or see him much. All my impression of him is that he's an extraordinary, very intelligent, and very violent guy. I don't know what direction his violence and rebellions take, but should guess that he might well be a Godsend so far as companionship is concerned at St. Andrew's. On the other hand, I know he is, to put it mildly, controversial: and perhaps you don't hit it off well at all. I hope you do. I'm sure at any rate he'll share most of your major feelings about the school.

I've been extremely busy on an article on machine-made rugs;* just finished a tentative draft; and am awaiting judgment, with time on my hands but naturally nervous time. I am thinking of applying for a

---

* "Sheep and Shuttleworths," *Fortune*, January, 1933, p. 43 (unsigned).

Guggenheim Fellowship, which would give me perfect freedom to write in France and $2500 to do it on, for as long as that would last—which should be quite a while, I think. But chances seem strongly against my getting it (they give preference to writers who have published and are of established reputation); and according to Mr. Canby (whom Mr. MacLeish consulted for me) it might even be rather tactless to apply before next year; meanwhile publishing all I can in magazines. MacLeish thinks I could do so in the *New Republic* and in the *Saturday Review*. Tomorrow I shall see the Guggenheim Secretary and see what he thinks the chances are of applying this year. The long poem is well liked and they are advising and I am eager to manage to get a job, stipend, or what not, which will make it possible to put much more time on it.

Via is entirely well and now lives in town, working on a magazine called *Symposium:* a part-time job which is pleasant and not tiring. We see each other as often as possible—which means fairly constantly— and everything seems well so far as we are concerned. I have a hideous trait of moodiness and worse which from time to time does bad things to both of us; but I'm trying as never before to understand, control it, or at worst control my reactions to it, and, thank God, am making some headway. It's the sort of intangible, slippery thing that I guess is worst in the world for two fairly nervous people to cope with; and when it's out of hand, neither of us has an easy time. I'm sometimes really forced to believe I have a dirty and unconquerable vein of melancholia in me; but I know this hypochondriacal feeling is the most dangerous imaginable to it. I know the most important faculty to develop is one for hard, continuous and varied work and living; but the difference between knowing this and doing anything consistent about it is often abysmal. Along with the melancholia, or a part of it, is rotten inertia and apathy and disgust with myself. However, I'm in very good spirits now.

My love to you and Mrs. Flye—

Rufus

Dear Father Flye:

A very happy New Year to you and to Mrs. Flye—and wish us one. Via Saunders and I will be married about the end of the month. I've meant for days to let you know—there's been the worst pressure yet at the office, to keep me from it. That has at least let up to some extent, leaving me, as you can easily enough see, thoroughly stupid and inert, with the Small Talk all leaked away and no brains or energy to write or even think any of the things I wish I could. I notice a good many things about becoming engaged and moving towards marriage that are sometimes tough to realize, but not really surprising. One is that you're no more subject to high feelings, gaiety, good cheer or sustained ecstasy about it than you'd be in becoming a priest or in writing a poem. From the outside it looks like a very simple and entirely pleasing matter, with no room for anything except Grade A happiness. It is, as a matter of fact, a definitely Serious Estate, and I couldn't enter into it lightly no matter how much I tried. The same goes for Via. My own misfortune is that Seriousness means Gloom to me, about half the time. Which God knows is hard on her. Another thing I notice is, that when you talk about it you talk about this as the gloomy side of it. The other side you understand better, and know other people do, and to put down We're-the-Happiest-People-in-the-World seems not only probably untrue but rather a private matter. It makes no difference what I notice, and I'd be glad not to notice things. The dirty part of it is that you write such a note as this and give people a fine impression of being really and consistently *un*happy about it. Which Heaven knows we are not.

We've already found an apartment, down near Uncle Hugh's, and Via's living in it now. A nice and unusually old house. We have two large basement rooms (this in case it's of any interest), a kitchen somewhat more roomy than they're likely to be in this hideous town, a broad and sheltered back porch, and a large yard with pool, large trees, incipient grass, flower beds and ivy. We'll be married Saturday, January 28th, in a church in Utica. Via wants to be confirmed. I'm advising her, (and she prefers, I think very rightly) to take her time with that—that is, to be converted and really very fully convinced in herself, rather than simply marrying into the church. We'd both be very grateful, as you know, if you'll remember us in your Mass that day.

Much love to you both,

Rufus

Dear Father Flye:

Thank you for your letter . . . We had a good vacation, but now that I'm back I'm up against trouble . . .

In the first place we have no money and I must earn a living. In the second, beyond that necessity I care very little about my job, except for my own writing and whatever may help me in it. In the third, the editor-in-chief was much impressed by my Tennessee Valley story* (which came out during my absence) and this morning called me and talked to me. He was as honest and as swell as anyone could wish for: my story was one of the best pieces of writing he'd ever seen in *Fortune*, but he knew I am weak on organization and that I understand business very poorly. On the strength of my usefulness as a writer, he is willing for me to stay on: but naturally on certain conditions: He will feed me tough business stories thick and fast: I must do my best to learn the business ropes: they shan't expect anything wildly fast out of me, but the idea is this: that I really am interested in doing well with this job: in making it a part of my career.—

He was certainly extremely direct and decent about it, and there were other reasons why I couldn't well say, when asked yes or no: "I'm not that much interested." One is that I'd much rather succeed than fail this job before I quit it. Another is that there's no other job in sight, and no other way of living except working. So I thanked him and said I'd work as hard and as much as possible.

But Lord knows with misgivings! They're very nice people to work for; much of the work in one way and another is interesting; but what it will profit me to become a good economist I don't see . . . Little writing

* "The Project Is Important," *Fortune*, October, 1933, p. 81 (unsigned).

as I've done, and little confidence as I've a right to, I still feel that life is short and that no other earthly thing is as important to me as learning how to write. And for that you *must* have time! I feel the well-known prison walls distinctly thickening: but if I should tell him honestly that side of the story, I'd be out of a job very soon. And then where? And how would I live? And what would happen to Via?

If I were as Quixotic as I feel, I'd quit today. And then I'd either starve or go stale tomorrow. I've no way of working out the problem. I have no idea what the path of least resistance is. If I find it, I don't know whether I'll take it. If I had as much confidence about writing as I have intention, everything might be much easier. But my confidence varies and is nil much of the time. Yet never little enough that I can even think of giving up writing.

Much love to you both,

Rufus

Dear Father Flye:

In two or three days, when I can get hold of another copy, I want to send you a copy of my book of poems,* not out of any pleasure in them myself but because I expect you would like to see and have them: if a dying man passed out his hair and his toenails to friends he would not be thought vain of hair, toenails, or his friendship. Not a dying man, and you are more than a friend, but the reason for all this elaborateness of diffidence is more genuine than it looks: I am in most possible kinds of pain, mental and spiritual that is. In this pain the book and its contents are a relatively small item, only noticeable in the general unpleasantness because they are tangible. The rest of the trouble is even more inexpressible, and a lot more harm, but revolves chiefly around the simple-sounding problem of how to become what I wish I could when I can't. That, however, is fierce and complicated enough to keep me balancing over suicide as you might lean out over the edge of a high building, as far as you could and keep from falling but with no special or constant desire not to fall. It works many ways: one is apathy, or a sort of leady, heavy silt that, always by nature a part of my blood, becomes thicker and thicker, and I, less pleasant and less bearable to live with, or to live within. Another is that without guidance, balance, coordination, my ideas and impressions and desires, which are much larger than I can begin to get to paper, are loose in my brains like wild beasts of assorted sizes and ferocities, not devouring each other but in the process tearing the zoo to parts. Or more accurately like the feeling they are loose wires highly charged which cross and short-circuit and send burning spasms all through me, with

* *Permit Me Voyage.* With a Foreword by Archibald MacLeish. No. 33 in the Yale Series of Younger Poets, Yale University Press, 1934.

nothing connecting long enough to hold, and give power or light. The wise answer of course would be that there is only one coordinator and guide, and that he is come at through self-negation. But: that can mean nothing to me until or unless I learn it for myself. Without scrupulousness I am damned forever, and my base, if I ever find it, must be of my own finding and understanding or it is no sort of base at all. Well, it cannot be solved. Not at any rate in process of this rotten letter. I can I think quite surely promise you that I shall not suicide. Also be sure I am sorry and ashamed for this letter, in every way but one, that being that between friends even the lowest cowardliness is not to be shut away and grinned about, if worse comes to worst. Aside from all these things, there is much to enjoy and more to be glad for than I deserve, and I know it, but they are mostly, by my own difficulty, out of my reach.

Much love to you and to Mrs. Flye,

R.

Dear Father Flye:

Pardon this morning's letter. But the present note is for more than to ask pardon. The idea fell into my head this noon, after absence of some months, of what possibilities there might be of teaching at St. Andrew's. For some time, and very much so lately, I have been sure I wanted, sooner or later and by preference sooner, to quit this job and all others that take much time, and definitely to concentrate on writing and on the amount of reading, talking, seeing and free time which are best needed to go into writing. An exceedingly hard problem, practically, because we have no money and must live and must even, before much more time has gone figure in what it would take to support a family. (Not that it's at all pressing.) In other words I must find ways to support life which will also be ways that will allow me a maximum amount of freedom. Hard combination. That is where the idea of St. Andrew's comes in. I would like to quit here, if I could, within a year, but can't be sure. In the first place do you think there would be a chance of my getting a job there? But that is at present less important to me than everything else about it. Here is the way it is to me: 1. I am attracted to teaching almost enough to dread it, but would in all ways predispose myself in coldness toward it: would use it only as a job which I would try to do well but would make no effort to break my heart over. 2. Would you guess, from your experience, that teaching at St. Andrew's would give me much and uninterrupted leisure? 3. Would you guess that I could do that sort of teaching (a) decently enough not to be shameful and (b) without cracking up nervously? I think I could but I know my weaknesses are many. 4. Especially important: how well do you think Via could manage? The whole thing would be as alien to her as anything that can be imagined, and though such changes for a harder life may be "good" for people, it depends on the people. She is an unusually gentle, sensitive and complicated person, by no means free of all the potentialities of melancholia and what have you, and it very seriously occurs to me that the life there might do her a great deal of harm. A heavy lot of questions to impose upon you, but for any answers whatever, I would be grateful.

Do you ever happen to see any of the Silly Symphonies by Walt Disney? On the whole they are very beautiful. A sort of combination of Mozart, super-ballet, and La Fontaine . . . Another thing to see, I hear, is *Men of Aran*.

Much love,
Rufus

[New York City]
Nov. 26 [1934]

Dear Father Flye:

Ran out of copies of the book* and of money at the same instant but am sending today, if I can get wrapping materials, a slightly damaged (returned from a borrower) copy. I am sorry for the damage and sorrier for the delay. And I am sorry for both the letters I sent you, which must have been troublesome. I should know better than to write letters in such states of mind, or worse. Yes even if there were room I would have reconsidered—in fact already had, on my own—the idea of teaching at St. Andrew's. A terrible idea, and very few redeeming features. I do as a matter of truth believe I could teach, and teach well; and that is one of the reasons I am so generally sure (to the point twice of avoiding following good chances for good jobs) that it would be very bad for me to

* *Permit Me Voyage.*

·teach. As for the badness of the writer teaching, I agree all the way; I also think but am not perfectly sure, that there is no job on earth that is not bad for the writer; including writing; and that he who must earn a living has got to take the disadvantages of any job for granted, and seek what advantages in each he can find. Again, though: every job is bad for him, but floating on blood-money can be even worse; killing. There really is no answer or solution and for want of one must say, live as you can, understand all you can, write when, all, and what you can. What we'll do when I quit here I have no idea. Am only sure I should quit. Possibly try to qualify ourselves through the next winter at Yaddo, a philanthropic art-colony near Saratoga. Anyway, to try to work hard enough not to care how or why you're living.

Have you read the Letters of D. H. Lawrence? You might be impatient with him or even bored by him, I don't know for sure. Think it very possible on other hand, you would enjoy and think very highly of him. He seems to me somewhat crazy all right, and certainly a man of genius, and I am at present convinced one of the greater and more nearly saintlike of people. No one certainly was ever more honest. There was a Frenchman whose name I forget, mid-19th century, who was chiefly the inventor of all the Nordic-supremacy tripe which Nietzche & Wagner advanced & Germany rots on now: when he was a younger and wiser man he made a tentative classification of human beings thus: Fils-du-Roi; Imbécile; Drôle; Brute. Sure it's slight and wrong, plenty of ways. It also has its interest, and good. Try fitting men & friends into it. Lawrence I think partook of all the lower three, but was most of all Imbécile, and all magnetized towards and almost partaking of Fils-du-Roi, which he must have believed he was. Beethoven a Fils by bootstraps; by nature a Brute-Imbécile, therefore a Drôle. Bach a born Fils; equal parts the other three. Shakespeare scarcely at all Brute; a born Fils, very much a Drôle, a most innocent Imbécile. Mozart about as pure Fils as ever lived; what wasn't Fils was Imbécile; the strains of Brute were those of a gentle, swift & small wild animal. His Drôle-ness all in the Imbécile level. Nijinski: Imbécile of very high almost kingly order. Galsworthy: a Drôle pure and simple. Whitman: Brute-Imbécile, demi-Fils. And so on. Rembrandt a Fils and Brute. Roosevelt a Drôle, so possessed by circumstance as to be almost Imbécile & to appear Fils by a few wide removes or series of mirrors. Lincoln one of the greatest and saddest of Drôles. So on. Leonardo practically unadulterated, ice-cold Fils; Michelangelo the most intense kind, and a mixture.

I hope Mrs. Flye is well and that you are . . . I want and mean to write more, but I'm bad at letters.

R.

[New York, June 6, 1935]

Dear Father Flye:

Thank you for your letter, very much, and for the poems . . . I am very glad to have the original Laurels poem,* which I'd never seen, and I think a great deal of the other one and shall make some tries at translating it. If the results are at all good I'll send it along. Housman made a very free translation indeed of the laurels: but that's all to the good if the result is: and I think his result is somewhere between good and great. It is the prefatory poem to the book he calls Last Poems. "We'll to the woods no more."

I hope you will like the TVA article—No: I don't really. Because I don't think much of it myself: glib, superficial & limited. Some half-good prose. I am managing by starts to get some writing done; am having some ideas for more extensive work.

* "Nous n'irons plus au bois, les lauriers sont coupés," by Théodore de Banville.

(2-3 days later—Wednesday in fact.)

Am not too sure of the content or nature excepting a general feeling that it will be pretty rough and pretty sore. For *Fortune*, I am now working on a story about Bookies (at horseraces), and Saratoga.* Difficult and one of very few interesting assignments I've had here. Different pieces of the day-night poem are scattered around in different hideouts downtown. I will mean to assemble them soon and type out and send you a copy. One thing I'm much interested in doing is a picture caption-chapter-head history of the United States. I am in no way qualified to do a real or impersonal history: this one would be as impersonal and "impressionistic" as a poem: and extremely jagged and crazy I think: a mixture of lyric, quotation, statistic and satire; essentially satire. The basic idea, technically, is one I think has still further possibilities: i.e. taking a body of facts which are very generally known in terms of very general traditions and conventions: assuming that your reader knows these facts (whether he does or not): and instead of expositing them, cutting in at the sharpest possible angles, and playing variants across their structure: essentially the same as (a) laying down a theme and (b) doing obscure variations on it: except that the theme —except as a subject, a general subject—is never stated. I made a start 2-3 years ago with a life of Jesus, using that general formula of the reader's knowledge, and telling the story in basic terms of Bruce Barton and liberal ministers, plus some of the more glib manners of Freud and a considerable use of Sunday-School dialects. Never finished it but it is a general manner which I think can work quite well. Hope so. Another idea: that in most present writing that is any good there is a strong consciousness of "anthropological" correctness, i.e. the writer takes

* "August in Saratoga," *Fortune*, August, 1933, p. 63 (unsigned).

great care, in writing of millhands, that they speak an exact Pittsburgh instead of Gary dialect; that no man should drive a yellow roadster with wire spokes who would not with scientific correctness be driving it—and so on and on. All of this I am for that matter a victim of, and I think there are excellent things about it. But: would it not be Freeing and Strengthening, both to the technic and to the Language—and to the mind of both writer and reader—if instead of this scientific-journalistic-scrupulousness, you should instead feel at liberty, say in a play, to develop a, say again, generic Workers' Language: in which, for instance, a Pgh millhand wd avail himself of cowboy slang, mountaineer idiom, racetrack jargon—anything under the sun which might in that instant most enforce his language. And then for that matter, break down your generics, so that there's only one: the spoken and natural language. And then break that down—say distinction between spoken and written language—so that there is simply the full language; a newseditor can use, then, sailortalk and the more technological slang of miners and liturgical phrases all in a sentence. Well: I don't know. The job a highly special environment plays in building a way of speech and a human being is too tremendous to think of garbling if you can help it: but there are all the same more essential ways of making a man's speech "in character."

Well. I've got to quit and work. Our love to you both—

R.

Dear Father Flye:

Short note in hour of too much weariness to manage to work on what I should be doing. Am assigned to rewrite a piece on orchids,* which could be a clear & inescapable small study of snobbism: but I can't catch it on the hip in the right way. The flower itself isn't responsible: but people's reactions to it have been and are so vile that I hate its very guts along with theirs. Of my own writing have been as usual trying this that and the other thing, finishing little or nothing. Most of it has hung somewhere between satire and what I suppose would be called "moralistic" writing: I wish I could get both washed out of my system and get anywhere near what the real job of art is: attempt to state things as they seem to be, minus personal opinion of any sort. No use talking: for various reasons of weakness & lack of time I continually fall far short of, i.e. betray, things I know better than to betray.

Very sick of summer and work in this city: usual heavy accretion over the brain of hurry & superficiality. This is a rotten note—I'm sorry for it. I may have asked before, not sure: have you read *La Condition Humaine* (André Malraux), *Voyage au Bout de la Nuit* (Ferdinand Céline) or *Fontamara* (Ignazio Silone)? All are in translation too & published here and all I think very far out of the class of any other books written right now. (The Malraux-English title is *Man's Fate.*) The Céline book is a good deal of Swift, Montaigne, Rabelais: practically pure horror from start to finish but horror written by the only kind of person who has a right: a person of absolute gentleness and honesty. I must try to get back to work. Starting this November, I get six months off:

* "The U. S. Commercial Orchid," *Fortune*, December, 1935, p. 108 (unsigned).

don't know yet where I'll go or whether, even, I'll leave town at all. Much love to you and Mrs. Flye.

Rufus

Dear Father Flye:

Thank you for your letter and for the poems. I have neither at hand right now and had not managed to determine what single one of the Voltaire stanzas* I liked best. I can though remember liking it a very great deal and also being somewhat surprised at it— this latter because I've read much too little of Voltaire to know at all what to expect. David's poem** is likable and moving as the first poems of Keats are to me—whether there's any such parallel in talent I don't know but only reasonably doubt. Which is vulgar, ridiculous & uncalled for but I do care not only that he should want to and enjoy continuing to write but for the writing as such. On that, excuse a few half-ideas. Most of the language and a good deal of the thought and feeling of the poetry is very naturally "literary"—which is the way & about the proportion it comes to nine out of ten writers bad or good or for that matter great, to start with—and from which Lord knows there is a lot to be learned. But also a great deal of harm to be absorbed which can be hard & even impossible to clear the head of. I was going to say I hope he can be talked with & shown the various & more important (in fact indispensable) other contents of poetry & of writing. But that is really stupid: except for certain & small pieces of help, those are either learned by yourself or not learned. But it has all caused me plenty of trouble,

* François-Marie de Voltaire, "À Madame du Châtelet."
** David McDowell, also an alumnus of St. Andrew's, and after Jim's death, the publisher of *A Death in the Family* and both volumes of *Agee on Film* (McDowell, Obolensky, 1957, 1958, 1960 respectively).

and is still doing that. My wish would be to save anyone else of it: but each person can only save himself:
I shouldn't have mentioned it. I'm glad of this possibility of his coming to Yale: God knows he deserves
it. No. Excuse my opinion which is both callow & only
personal: he deserves everything which can open clear
& sharpen his appetite and feed it, and I don't know
at all that that is best to be had at Yale or Harvard
though at such places it does exist in concentrated as
well as in disguised forms. I'm not such a dope as to
think I or anyone can find his own way unassisted
but the more of that and the less guidance & elabora-
tion of the means, the better. College elaborated a lot
of things out of recognition for me and that was
partly but only partly my limitations, immaturity, etc.
Thinking of it now I would give anything to have had
access to a good library and perhaps also to lectures,
and to friends & acquaintances of all sorts & to have
let it go at that. But that's wishful & probably roman-
ticized feeling. Probably I'd have thought no more
clearly and used time no better than I did. And do.
Phooey. I really deserve to have no opinions. But I
wish only best luck to David, whatever that may
mean or be, and will you give him my best.

I hadn't realized that I hadn't before mentioned my
furlough. Begins in November, runs through to May.
Plans are still unclear. Just conceivably, I will take a
new part-time job doing a review column for a magazine called *News-Week*, in which case the leave would
be off; I would quit *Fortune* and stay here. That depends, though, on the job definitely opening (it is
now hanging fire); on whether it would pay enough
to sustain life (which is not at all certain); on whether
it would consume relatively little enough time to allow
real concentration on my own writing (which it seems
it might). And to some extent on just how badly, at
the last minute, I might want six months' complete
free time. If these things all cleared I think I'd take it:

but I doubt if they clear. If they don't, we are all but certain now that we will get out of town for the leave. We have been offered a house in the country in northwest Connecticut, and we may go there. More likely though, we'll break drastically out of the whole vicinity. Everything within a hundred-mile radius of NYC seems thudding and over-populated, a sort of suburb of this town—even the open country: and New England seems to have been lived-in by so many people the soil is in all ways exhausted. All of which is oversensitive but has all the same some literal meaning to me. I think we would come South or go to the Midwest but where, am not at all sure. We had thought of getting a cottage or what somewhere near you, and still do think of that. I think though that probably the first few months would better be spent alone—get a certain bulk of work under the belt, if possible, before. I'm likely to get restless & to diffuse too much in talk if I have half a chance, and I do want instead, if I'm at all able, to spend the time getting writing done. Whether I can or will or not, God only knows. Much of the time I doubt it. But again my general hope & idea is that by middle March or by April I will have enough stuff done to feel anyway that I've made a beginning. And I hope then, that we can live near enough to see you a lot. My plans in all directions, you can see, are very vague indeed: but any tightening of them would be faking, right now anyhow.

About the orchid. It is silly of me I know to dislike the flower as such: it is not responsible. I think probably I dislike it by transference: because I do much dislike the kinds of people who like it and their reasons for liking it: liking a thing because it is the Largest, the Loudest, the Most Expensive, the most supercharged with Eroticism, Glamor, Prestige—I don't like. Automatically thinking a thing is beautiful for such reasons I like even less. As a commodity, and that is the way I'm supposed to write of it, it is more completely endowed with snob-appeal and with nothing else, than any other commodity I know of. And then for that matter I just privately don't like the plain looks of the flower. Any flower is built of course for one special purpose: to propagate itself: of any flower, the private parts and the face are one & the same, and that seems more than all right to me: but it does seem to me that the orchid abuses the privilege. "The orchid gets its name from the Greek *orchis*, which means testicle; and there are those who condemn that title as understating the case, since to them the flower resembles nothing printable so much as a psychopathic nightmare in technicolor. It has also been favorably compared in sexual extravagance to the south apse of an aroused mandrill, and it sports a lower lip that qualifies to send the Bourbon Dynasty into green visceral spasms of invidious love's labors lost." And so, "though not a single promotive gesture had been made over the orchid throughout all the centuries up to 1929, the orchid was already, in the minds of many select ladies and gentlemen who could afford to have the idea, a very definite if sort of Special last word, if it was a last word you wanted to touch off the establishment of a young woman as at liberty for marriage, or most gracefully and with most conspicuous expense to assert your opinion of her as something pretty nice to be seen with, or to set her off at her virginal sweetest as she was wedded in unsunderable wedlock, or indeed to lend Class to any occasion of social or sentimental stature such as the celebration, by snotting one's neighbor along Fifth Avenue, of the embarrassment and ultimate destruction of Death through the glorious resurrection of Jesus Christ." That was written for but will probably not be included in the orchid ms.

I have for the present been transferred to a rush job

on Modern Interiors,* complicated by the fact that of four leading decorators *Fortune* commissioned to design their ideas of a modern room, only one has anything remotely to do with anything definable as 'modern.' About like being assigned to do an article on aerodynamics and having to illustrate it with pictures of streamlined fountain-pens, ashtrays & water-closets—with one airplane tossed in as an afterthought. Not that I feel specially excited about the home as a Machine for Living.

Long's assassin was a brave man, but there were more deserving people to die killing. Hearst might head a purely local list but if you weren't being provincial about it I guess Hitler would nose him out. Hitler and several of his friends. I have thought how interesting and serviceable it would be to organize a group of terrorists: say 600 young men who don't care especially for their lives: to pair them off to trail the 300 key sonsofbitches of the earth (if they were that glibly easy to select): and exactly a year from then, at just the same hour all over the world, to ring up the assassinations. But I don't really qualify at all: I doubt it would do more good than harm: and you would certainly kill a good many innocent men, not all of them bystanders.

Love to you both. We look forward to seeing you.
Rufus

* "What D'You Mean, Modern?", *Fortune*, November, 1935, p. 97 (unsigned).

Anna Maria, Florida
26 December [1935]

Dear Father and Mrs. Flye:

Thank you so much for the note and for the card. Christmas is so good a time, the excuses seem very small why feelings, any day in the year, should not be the same. I remembered you both read stories of Chekhov with father and mother and liked them, so sent the plays, which I love—they are good when you feel like it to read aloud—better that way than silent I think. Like especially *The Three Sisters* and *The Cherry Orchard*. I was given among other things *The Dog Beneath the Skin*, and look forward to reading it with you in the Spring. Have also been reading Van Gogh's letters to his brother—believe you'd like them too—and Blake's *Songs of Innocence*. So cold here the past ten days there's hardly any use being here. Everyone says it's abnormal: probably abnormal like static in radio or an appetite. Well there's sure to be some warm weather: we've seen some samples. I feel very dumb and must quit and try to get to work. Excuse this dull note, and much love to you.

Rufus.

Dear Father Flye:

Thank you a lot for your letter, which I'd like to have answered by now several times over, but was and am as usual in a state of eagerness to communicate but of atrophy in all ways of doing it. Sorry for that matter to sit around describing States, but I guess it's about all I'm capable of. The states of feeling, &c, go up and down in me anyhow a good deal, without much consistency except a too constant anxiety or fear: not on the whole especially happy, or more than a fraction alive spiritually, and certainly seldom productive of any good, inside or outside me. I wish there were less self-pity in that than there probably is: I just know that I have a terrible amount to learn, unlearn, reclaim and discipline in myself, and have at the same time a feeling of having somewhere through ignorance & cowardice switched, without knowing it onto another track, which may be a track leading somewhere but which leads into a part of the world, or a world, which doesn't happen to be the one I value. You would (not in any officiousness heaven knows but in faith) be able to tell me where and how I have switched off and how things are retrievable or correctible, and I wouldn't deny you, but then again I doubt if I could believe it. Things have to be believed with the body or in other words soul, not just perceived of the mind. It has seemed reasonable and true for a long time to me (to the mind) that a life is found only in losing it, but what I take to be my actual organic flesh and soul is only at the very beginning of realizing that as true (as if the truth were now just moved in beyond the torn edge of a blotter), and it can mean nothing to me until they are absorbed in it. I care mainly about just 2 things. Sometimes they seem identical or at least like binary stars, & sometimes they seem like a split which can completely destroy. They would be (1) getting as near truth and whole truth as is humanly possible, which means several sorts of 'Truth' maybe, but on the whole means spiritual life, integrity and growth; and (2) setting this (near-) truth out in the clearest and cleanest possible terms. And I feel about it in two ways which may or may not be identical; one is I believe genuine 'hunger' toward it, and the other, if it is another, is ambition, which I think would kill it. It doesn't happen in its worst levels to be 'worldly' ambition (though I have bad streaks of that too), but is probably more intense and destructive because it isn't. I shouldn't have said 'if it is another'; I know it is. A general feeling of very much preference to die if I fail in the things I want (or fail at least to come near enough them to 'justify' going on living). So there's a pretty strong undertone of cold fear or despair which is false or at least of a false kind and irrelevant, and which doesn't often leave and at times completely occupies me. It looks to me as if one, maybe the first, of several main jobs of self-clearance and self-discipline I must undertake, is getting rid of that, and that of course involves getting rid of the things which cause it; some of which must be ambition and pride, which if you have are bound to make you cross-eyed to the truth. This sort of thing is hard and probably mistaken to write about, but I look forward to talking about them and a good many less Desperate affairs this Spring. There are a couple of things I'd like to say—can't probably say them but will try to indicate them anyway. I know there are two things about me that inevitably must cause you pain and annoyance, perhaps anger, and that keep us from being able to talk easily and really fully. One is sophistication or cynicism and the other is communism. The first (call it cynicism for short) I think I was probably beginning to absorb about the time we were last able to see each other much, the trip to Europe; and I've steadily taken a lot of it aboard ever since. I don't mean to be psychologically glib, but I think I know one reason: it's a defense and therefore an indication and encourager of cowardliness. I'm not now and wasn't then any wow of private strength or wisdom, and it was almost chemically necessary to the kind of growing-up that I, a certain kind of person, had. I got a very thick crust of it and it is one of the strongest habits of mind (my mind that is) & one of its strongest appetites now, and of course either governs or shows itself in one 'reaction' after another. It's a bad and smug trait in plenty of ways, but it isn't necessarily entirely that. I don't think I'm trying to defend it or myself but only to explain that many kinds of remarks I make, etc. are not so facilely or hatefully brought about as they may seem—that if some whole set of things becomes something of which in its details I seem pretty glibly scornful, that all the same comes out of a good deal of not so cynical effort to understand what that set of things means. I'm not claiming to be honest, because I realize that I'm not, but I do swear that I want to be and try to be: and that makes you angry against things, including yourself, which are not honest: and when (like, say Will Hays) one of them appears so to you for a long enough time, your anger and scorn become automatic. The same with things which appear useless or cruel even though honestly convinced, like the Roosevelt administration or plenty of the processes of Stalin. And so on.

The same with communism. I'm not an economist and I haven't done and probably won't do all the Reading, but I promise you I'm not so glib of it as you are bound to think. I'm pretty sure I'll never be one, and there are things about it I despise. But there are things all through the world as it is that look to me bad, and there are many things in that set of ideas which look to me good; and I think more of them may conceivably succeed than we have any cynical right to think. Well, with that too, though as I say I'm not informed at the sources etc. there are a great many ways I feel convinced beyond a need to get further into the sources. I didn't at all get convinced over night. It was three years of exposure to foulness through *Fortune* and the general News, and of reading, thinking, talking and so forth. I don't mean to say that I think I've found out the answers so far as I think they concern me, but an awful lot of things do seem somewhere near and right from that, or essentially that, point of view, as the same things don't from any other. I'm not totally obsessed with it but it is a good deal of my mind and it does seem important, so that I'm bound both to write and to talk about it. I don't feel so bigoted as you think. Their bigotry is one of the things I dislike about them. I haven't a better friend in the world than you and I can't stand misunderstandings of any kind that shut between that. When I'm eager to talk with you on this subject, any eagerness to 'convert,' if or when it is there at all (and I guess it is) is the very least of the reasons why. One reason is a natural friendly eagerness to communicate on things which mean a lot to me—Another is, a difference of belief on a subject of that size runs deep and involves a lot of things, and it does seem extremely important that the beliefs and the reasons for them be mutually and thoroughly understood: which takes the worst harm out of any disagreement. If in the course of talking about it you should see too that there is some sense in it, I'd be glad. But even though I would be glad, that is secondary to understanding, and a long way secondary. I would care more than I can tell if we could both put aside or at least 'delay' on this and maybe other subjects, for God knows I know your goodness and hope and believe you trust my sincerity: and let a lot of these things work themselves out. I think I'm being over-something-or-other—that with time, which we'll have and have lacked for so long, they'll do that without any such talking as this.

Do you know the writing of J W N Sullivan? (on science mostly.) I've just read one, *Beethoven: His Spiritual Development*, which I think very fine, and am reading *Science: a New Outline*, which seems so too. Wrote a poem the evening of the night the King died, on his death. I don't think much of it but would like to show it to you. Much love to you and Mrs. Flye.

Rufus.

[*Anna Maria, Fla.*]
[*March 13, 1936*]

Dear Father and Mrs. Flye:

Thanks so much for the letters. Glad the weather is good at last. It is here, too, in general—very violent North wind today, but almost a warm one even so. Please don't mind the total vacuousness of this—I've been having accesses of work lately which I've now either lost or am for the time being exhausted out of —in either case it leaves me with an empty head and hardly the literal physical energy to put down one word after the other. The more or less "pressing" thing I want to write about is our coming up—the clearest I can make out now is, we might be arriving shortly before Easter; or towards end of April—just conceivably later—Saw the new Charlie Chaplin a while back. If it comes and if it doesn't conflict with Lenten rule, it's a wonderful thing to see—a lot, to me, as if Beethoven were living now and had completed another symphony. Very little reading lately: combined hard work and inertia. Father, have you read much of André Gide and if so what do you think of him? V. has been reading 2 or three—*Symphonie*

Pastorale, La Porte Étroite: I've read only *Les Faux-Monnayeurs* (in English). Think he's a pretty fine writer. Am enclosing a short poem: would I suppose be described as an intended sort of Christian-Communist morning hymn, as sung probably in America. Time keeps shortening and I look forward more and more to time on the mountain.

Much love to you both,

Rufus.

Dear Father and Mrs. Flye:

(excuse the card, this is hurried) We'll be leaving here Wednesday the 15th and (unless floods should come and get dangerous) will go to New Orleans and up the river. May stop couple days in N.O. On a rough guess would think we'd arrive around the 25th: will of course keep you posted ahead of arrival. Very naturally you might wonder about *Fortune* and time limit: I never made it very clear. As it turned out I made no "leave-of-absence" arrangement, but only one by which I can do articles when I need the money; so it isn't necessary to get back by 1 May: though I can't dally away forever: will begin to need money again. It will be so swell to see you. Am reading *The Golden Bough:* a pretty wonderful book (the 1-volume edition, not the 12-volume); and lately have had (at last) the sense to spend some time outdoors: which is a good thing all around. The weather: wonderful now, and there have been days and evenings of a kind I've never seen the like of elsewhere: like honey if latter were breathable and weren't sticky. Much love for you both—

Rufus

Dear Father:

Thank you for both your letters and particularly for the first: I believe you will know how much it means to me—and how fully I return and feel its contents myself. I like Weigall a great deal; seems to be one of fairly few scholars who can (and takes care to) write with real beauty and flexibility & feeling: and vice versa, haven't seen the June *Mercury:* have read in it things of Huefferford Madoxford before: or one: one on Stephen Crane. Ford can certainly at times write and does certainly at times have fine ideas & 'reactions': at other times he irks me quite a lot (vide his terrific sideslip towards superlatives: a favorable comparison of S. Crane with Shakespeare: vide also certain diminutives of a sort I can ill bear in or out of print except when In Character: calling or mentioning Crane, over and over, as Steevie, and as Poor, dear, wild little Steevie.) Glad to be out of that morass of parenthesis. Would add, on Ford: he is very fond of using what Englishmen think of as the American language, and has less ear on it than anyone since Galsworthy and, if you bar G., since The Venerable Bede. Am curious and eager to read the Webb work:* we are in fact thinking of clubbing in with another indigent family & buying it. It does sound to be far more impartial and infinitely more solidly documented than anything on subject to date. Curious also what *Mercury* review was of it. *Mercury*'s present general slant is one which particularly enrages me, less because it is anti-red and sometimes rather strongly pro-fascist than because it is time and again patently uninformed on its reactions and tries to sound definitive on them. But that of course proves nothing about individual pieces in it.

Later: I must cut this short and do a week's work in

* Sidney and Beatrice Webb, *Soviet Communism: A New Civilization?* (Scribner, 1936).

next 20 hours or so: have been assigned to do a story on: a sharecropper family (daily & yearly life): and also a study of Farm Economics in the South (impossible for me): and also on the several efforts to help the situation: i.e. Govt. and state work; theories & wishes of Southern liberals; whole story of the 2 Southern Unions. Best break I ever had on *Fortune*. Feel terrific personal responsibility toward story; considerable doubts of my ability to bring it off; considerable more of *Fortune*'s ultimate willingness to use it as it seems (in theory) to me. Will be starting South Saturday. For a month's work. Will count strongly on seeing you if only for few hours . . . Don't as yet know when of course. Will keep you posted. I agree with Mrs. Flye: no time or visit ever, anywhere, has been so good and meant so much to me. Much love to you both.

Rufus

Am reading by degrees a very good biography of Dostoevsky, by Avram Yarmolinsky: and a novel called *The Castle*, by a German-Bohemian-Jew Franz Kafka: a great though limited reputation in Europe as one of not more than 3 writers of the century; book spoken of as a contemporary *Pilgrim's Progress;* which among other things it is, with such differences as these: Christian always knew: this will be tough but if I do thus and so (and I know exactly what) I will come through all right. Here: in *The Castle*, it is more difficult: the pilgrim though he knows there is a destination that means more than his life to him, is not at all sure what is there, or what to do to get there; and learns that not only his own efforts to find out what to do, how to live, can give him no sure answer, but that he must by no means entirely trust the advice of older inhabitants. Book full of terrific ambiguities and half-lights, a certain amount also of irony, but on whole very far above altitude of irony. Wonderful job I think. Am also now doing good deal of re-writing & typing of winter's work, which begins to look somewhat better than I had thought it was—I don't know yet. Also am anxious to get to work on a new Englishing of libretto for Gluck's *Orpheus:* a terrible job. Probably shall not have a chance again now till September. Certainly am landing in a swirl of work. Have you ever heard or heard of Mitchell's Christian Singers (Recorded by Melotone)? They sing for dimes around Winston-Salem, take a busride to N.Y. a couple of times a year, record their spirituals, which sell only in the deep south, and get back on their bus-seats, unhonored and unsung. They are the greatest singers of spirituals I've ever heard recorded: in fact I dread all other recordings I've ever heard: latter all full of orotundity, training, self-conscious-ness, selfconscious unselfconsciousness, and a pathetic and repellent mah-people attitude. These men are as pure of that whole business as glass. Hear records of them when & if you can. *Must* quit now. Love

R.

Dear Father and Mrs. Flye:

I feel pretty thoroughly sick of myself over my failure to communicate further to you anything definite about our seeing you when we were in the south. Everything there was unpredictable from day to day, I was half crazy with the heat and diet, and I lost all imagination of how, having heard from me that I would show up, you might have been waiting for word and even discarding or postponing other plans. Well there is nothing I could or would say for myself—only that I am much sorrier than I can tell you. The trip was very hard, and certainly one of the best things I've ever had happen to me. Writing what we found is a different matter. Impossible in any form and length *Fortune* can use; and I am now so stultified trying to do that, that I'm afraid I've lost ability to make it right in my own way. Well, I don't know.

Have you read *The Edwardians*, Victoria Sackville-West? A *very* good book. Have been reading, too, stories by the young English poet Stephen Spender, and a book of criticism by him, *The Destructive Element*. Latter seems as good as any contemporary criticism I know of. One of his leading convictions is that Henry James is a very great writer, and one who is responsible for much or most of the best English writing since. Compares him with Beethoven. No movies that are any good at all. None at any rate that I want to see except as movie history: such as *Romeo and Juliet*, which from all I see of it in stills and read about it is exactly the most pernicious sort of production I can think of: every thing which is dead against all that the movies could best be, done solidly enough to draw a great deal into its whirlpool which might otherwise be good or developing toward good. It isn't a question of the movies desecrating Shakespeare but of Shakespeare desecrating the movies: at any rate the sort of Shakespeare who reaches the movies; so choked with Reverence and Scholarship and all the embalming fluids of the past 300 years that no glint of life is left in it. I must quit and get back to work. Much love to you and again my self-disgust.

Rufus

[New York City]
[January 20, 1937]

Dear Father:

Thank you and Mrs. Flye for your letter. A good year to you and much love. As I read further into it I keep wondering whether I've asked you and whether you have read and if so whether or how much you like the work of Marcel Proust which I am now reading (in English, what seems a very fine translation). I have an idea you would both care as much for him as I do: I can't imagine there has ever been a more complete taking apart of states of consciousness. That's all I'm reading just now—there are 4 volumes of it and I'm in the 2nd. Seems a sad year for movies and a boring one on the stage. Some good Art Shows of which I've not seen much—but was very much moved by the big Fantasy and Surrealism Show and the 2 Picasso shows. A book will be coming out in 2 or 3 months which I hope you will see and think you will like. I've read the author's* first book (*Fontamara*) and the first few chapters of this one (called *Bread and Wine*) in manuscript and think them both, great and beautiful pieces of writing. This second, so far as I saw it, is the solidest piece of writing I have seen bringing through the ideas we were talking of about Christianity and Communism.

* Ignazio Silone.

I am doing some writing but not what I should be doing: I seem to be lazy, and badly organized, beyond any idea I had had of it, and am going to have to get violent with myself.

Much love to both of you,

Rufus

[New York City]
[November 26, 1937]

Dear Father:

Thank you for your letter, and for your letter of a short while back. The world (and my self) seem to me this morning, in light of recent context, evil, exhausting and hopeless, not to mention nauseating and infuriating and incurable, yet I am thoroughly glad I am in it and alive. I would probably do well to be this tired all the time, for I am slowed and weighted enough to be in palpable and strong connection. An excess of vitality can evidently be a great spiritual handicap: most of the time I feel full enough of electricity or gas that I feel off the ground, over-rapid and substanceless . . .

Bierce is good. I have a long time wanted to read *The Devil's Dictionary* whole. Irony and savage anger and even certain planes of cynicism are, used right, nearly as good instruments and weapons as love, and not by any means incompatible with it; good lens-wipers and good auxiliaries. In plenty of ways I care most for those who lack the easing and comfort of direct love, Swift above any; and a lot for smaller, sharp intelligent soreheads like Bierce. *Franz Kafka* is a wonderful writer, to me a truly and intensely religious one as Blake and Dostoevsky were and as Joyce is; but more directly than Joyce. In a way totally uninterested in 'literature' or 'art' except in so far as they are his particular instrument for studying, questioning and suggesting more sharply than he otherwise could. I feel sure you would care for his books. They are *The Trial* (Knopf), *The Castle* (in England, Gollancz) and *The Great Wall of China* (Gollancz). Bierce's aphorisms, and recent reading of Kafka brought Kafka to mind . . .

Much love to you and Mrs. Flye. I'm glad you liked the *Cruise* article* for I feel sure you know its cruelty was used to inspire pity in readers who never feel it when it is asked in another's behalf directly. I would like to do the same article over more fully, and better. I never intend to write at all *steadily* for another again unless it is a hundred per cent work I want to do and believe in for itself. That I am quite sure is impossible. I will work for money only when I have to have it and think security and solidity and respect for these hopeless and murderous traps and delusions.

R.

* "Six Days at Sea," *Fortune*, September, 1937, p. 117 (unsigned).

Dear Father:

. . . I have only a dim and uninformed impression of Cordell Hull; from such as I have I feel a consistent but unlike you a qualified respect for him. Of the respect I think it must be much what your own is: respect for him as a strong and unusually constant kind of Christian and gentleman and statesman, in good meaning of these words, and a liking for the fact that these things show themselves in a good deal of beauty and purity of demeanor; and a feeling of him as one of the more excellent and characteristic kinds of Americans; a person who would inevitably have come from the land, and in many essences, from land and climates and mental and spiritual climates of this country as differing from another. This respect is qualified in ways which I probably can't succeed in making sound superior to glib, youthful and impudent, but I will try, feeling there are better things in it: not of my invention or nature, but in the body or conception of "truth" or "goodness" as a whole. But I shan't at all succeed in saying coherently what I mean or believe, for I would have to write or talk volumes indicating why I believe it; also, I am far less convinced that I know anything coherent and positive other than this, that or the other is misled, compromised or useless: in other words, much of my "conviction" is negative. But what little I can say, is this: I am essentially an anarchist, with the belief that the operations of human need and acquisitiveness, in concentration on purely material necessities and half-necessities, and the structures of law through which these operations are canalized, restrained and governed: that all this is tragic, mistaken and eccentric from the root up, and cannot come to good; and that the effort to manipulate for good within such a framework, no matter how sincerely, can only result in

compromise; and can finally or even in detail add only
to a sum total of evil, misfortune, and misapplication
of human energy towards goodness. I can conceive
of this: that a person who would wish to know and
do good "realistically" accept the human situation at
the worst that it is and work within and in terms of
its physique, with patience and understanding, and
doubt of himself as well as of all else; but those who
do this in the name of "realism" seem invariably to
capitulate, to shift their centre from absolutes to relatives, and in so doing to corrupt their own effort,
inevitably, and usually without knowing it. In other
words, compromise could be permissible *only* if what
was compromised were remembered as far more important to be striven towards than any thing which
has been only in part achieved; and over and over
this seems to be impossible. So that one is led completely to prefer the Absolutist, the person who regards only the literal, the nearest approach to the
total. For instance, Francis of Assisi seems to me violently to have restored ideas of Jesus: of complete
disregard for the structures of the world or of living
as it was: but this was modified by his disciples even
during his lifetime, so that it could exist in the world
among people with less spiritual energy. I would say
then: that the full literal Christian idea has no regard
for existence in the world as it is, but only for its own
existence, and that it is of a sort which would destroy
the structure of the world as it is, in proportion to
how generally and how uncompromisedly it was fol-
lowed. That it is *utterly* destructive to *any* contentment with the "things of the world" as they stand, and
can find or approach contentment only within the
purity of its own terms; and that any organization
whether of material or of belief which seeks to sub-
stantiate it in the "world as is" and there to make it
amenable or acceptable can only result in betrayal of
its essence: hence I feel bound to be an anarchist in

religion as well as "politics" and to feel that the effort toward good in both is identical, and that a man who wants and intends good cannot afford to have the slightest respect for that which is willing to accept itself as it is, or to be pleased with a "successful" compromise. For such reasons all politics would be corrupt from the ground up, with the tragic complication that good is enlisted in the cause of evil and that sincerity is almost the most destructive virtue of all. So again, I was not fully veracious when I said "Christian, gentleman, and statesman in good senses of the words," for I could mean at best only good relative to the evil structure of the world; whereas, relative to "absolute," which I feel can be the only centre, I could feel only that Hull is excellent only to the degree that his consciousness can let him be; that in some important respects his consciousness is not highly developed; and that if it were, he could not be Secretary of State, good, bad, or indifferent. Sorry for all this. If I could make even what confused little I believe clear, you would know it came from better sources than the mere arrogance or impudence it must seem to.

It was for such reason too, that I didn't read the articles you recommended in the *Saturday Evening Post*, that I felt they were on a subject—i.e. government—which was not good enough at best. I felt personally badly about this, for I didn't want to seem to you either careless or bigoted, but I knew through your enthusiasm for them that there must be excellence in them; but I could not get excited, because it seemed certain to me that this goodness or intelligence focused itself around and respected a set of values and conceptions which seem to me (simply because they are Government As Is) to be eccentric and thus inevitably inimical to human good.

At the same time I feel more shaken, confused, and ignorant, through my own actions, than I can remember having felt before. Yet my sense of confusion, ignorance, guilt and disintegrity is not to be cured by reversing and betraying such few things as in all faith and vigilance and scepticism not only of authority but of myself, still seem to me to be so. Quite plainly I know that in the most important things, or many of them, in my existence, I cannot know for sure what I am doing, or why, or at all surely the difference between right and wrong, which latter very often appear to be identical or so interlocked that the destruction of one entails the destruction of the other, like separating Siamese twins who use the same heart and bloodstream. This may simply mean that he who moves beyond the safety of rules finds himself inevitably in the "tragedy" of the "human situation," which rules have been built to avoid or anaesthetize, and which must be undertaken without anaesthetic: but I am suspicious of laying pity and grief and sadness to such a general, fatal source rather than to a source for which I am personally responsible.

I have a great deal of Puritan in me. I both despise it and am seized by it, and I know that I do not understand it, or myself, and that I am not sure but what Puritanism is the slickest disguise of the greatest of the earthly devils. I know that above all I believe in joy and in purity and fearlessness of soul, and that Puritanism seems rather more inimical than friendly to any known approach to this: and I know my effort has been and is towards goodness and true thinking and conduct and against rationalization; and I suppose it is only in knowledge of my "sincerity," (that again damnable and limiting word) that I can feel any integrity, or basis for peaceful and clear living and work. But I know also that the most dangerous rationalizations are unconscious and indivisible, and that if no one is superior to these, then certainly I am not.

Of marriage, sexual love, how or whether two or

more people are to spend time or a lifetime together, I feel most essentially that I know nothing whole but only untrustworthy fragments; also, that nobody else knows any more than that, pro, con, or in between. Again, much of what little I think I know is negative. I feel sure that not only the social but the religious structures and conceptions on these subjects are evil beyond imagination of the massiveness of the pain and stultification they have caused; though the essence of the religious idea, enlisted in the cause of hatred, impurity, and cowardice, is of itself no such thing but perhaps the most nearly "true" there is: and that is, of sexual love as a sacrament and one of the close centres of existence. But the conceptions of chastity are to my very best effort to understand them most abominably cancelling of this "sacramental" fact, and utterly unchaste, and productive only of ruin and pollution . . .

Goodbye and much love to you, and to Mrs. Flye.

Rufus

P.S. This is now several days later. If this seems bad, annoying, ill-tempered or otherwise no good please forgive it.

Dear Father:

It was good to hear this morning. I've been so deeply sucked into work that I've been lonely, rather than satisfied in the work, in which I cannot be satisfied as it is going. This I doubt will be much more than a flat note, for I'm pretty stupid with work and am writing this as a slightly guilty vacation from it. I'd like to think a good deal more and talk with you rather than writing, of law and of what you wrote of it. I'm pretty well aware, though not I expect aware enough, of the dependencies and good functions you speak of, and have a feeling that by and large the legal structure stitches together into something which insecurely functions, but *does function alive*, the weltering madhouse or cage of wild beasts and vipers, and has to be given this credit or respect. It is also a machine by which the lives of a majority are regularly and permissibly ground out for the uses of others: that, quite aside from its main corruptions. My feeling towards it is pretty thoroughly amoral: I will enjoy every advantage it yields me which I can be sure does not hurt another or others or to whatever degree I feel it is granted to others, and will obey it when as is of course so on some important counts it happens to coincide with my own conscience, and will show surface-obedience when disobedience would be troublesome or painful to me out of proportion to the value of public statement in action of the idea or ideal I am disagreeing on: but in any judgment of human conduct or "rights" I do not trust or respect it for five minutes as against my own, rudimentary as I feel my own to be, and I am a frenetic enemy against authority and against obedience for obedience's sake, and against "society" insofar as "society" is content with itself. I would not at all work to lose for myself or others such defenses or conveniences even as have been gained, but I am much more concerned in the ways in which all people appear still to be defenseless, against poisons much more sinister than physical danger: and these the structure of law and belief and obedience very greatly encourage. If there were a law which condemned every school I know of as a lethal chamber, and another which interdicted the use of all words to which the reader cannot give a referent, and another which established a staff whose constant vigilance was an analysis and rectification of the corruption of facts and ideas through miscommunication, and of the inevitable tendency of all authority to crystallize and petrify; and so on; and so on; and another which disbarred any lawyer or judge who made use of precedent; and so on; that would be a little more like it; though I will grant it would be even more steeply subject to misuse.

My writing is in bad shape. The past five weeks have been completely sterile and I've just gotten a postponement of publication until the middle of winter and so, till November or December for more work, but even so I am in trouble, near the bottom of borrowed money. The book* as I may have told you is a short one on the three tenant families Walker and I know in Alabama: thirty-two photographs and seventy-five thousand words (about 200 pages). My trouble is, such a subject cannot be seriously looked at without intensifying itself toward a centre which is beyond what I, or anyone else, is capable of writing of: the whole problem and nature of existence. Trying to write it in terms of moral problems alone is more than I can possibly do. My main hope is to state the central subject and my ignorance from the start, and to manage to indicate that no one can afford to treat any human subject more glibly or to act on any less would-be central basis: well, there's no use trying to

* Let Us Now Praise Famous Men (Houghton Mifflin, 1941, 1960).

talk about it. If I could make it what it ought to be made I would not be human.

I feel as I were disintegrating and "growing up," whatever that means, simultaneously, and that there is a race or bloody grappling going on between the two in my head and solar plexus. I would like to learn how to be relieved of such pain and poison as is not necessary, and how to stand that which is inevitable. I trust much but not enough in psychoanalysis, which I could not afford even if I believed in it fully enough to subject myself to it. I trust nothing else save a feeling of God, and love, and in part myself, but here too I know my ignorance is such that I am handling and eating medicines and poisons blindfold and indiscriminate. It seems to me very dangerous to be alive save through denials of the main point of living, the effort to understand such as you can, and to live and work accordingly. I could mainly care for innocence and devotion, but that is qualified when you see innocence eat its own death and ruin and devote all its life and fierceness to it. But I should guess it is only through the persistence of this quality, if it is also innocent enough never to believe what it is told, nor to be aware of or to mind the danger of not doing so, that any better or further future will be opened up. This is mainly nonsense. I am too much the born Liberal, or Reasonable Man. I doubt there is any bumbling with rationality in the world I most believe in and most want to become of, but a good deal of joy, fire and kindness in its place. I wish I might see you and I wish this book was done. Much love to you and to Mrs. Flye.

R.

Did you read of the young man on the hotel ledge in New York? Who went out there desiring to be alone from a room of female relatives? He stayed there eleven hours, with the room occupied on one side and the whole city gawping up from below him, and between these pressures, from which apparently none thought twice of relieving him, he finally jumped. A man who stands on a ledge eleven hours and drinks coffee does not want to die. I think the situation is a perfecting into literal symbolism of a routine which is suffered by every young man who will not capitulate: he capitulates all the same in madness or in death; or just very occasionally through craft, talent or cruelty, bursts the trap; but if so, its marks are on him, forever.

Father: I am at the postoffice. I became involved in what I was talking of and only now remember the other things which in fact mean more to me: that I do realize your understanding and sympathy, and know we need never fear to speak openly. As I now speak of it it seems flatly realized, and I can't say more of it now, but I believe you know how greatly I value it.

Dear Father:

Thank you very much for your letter. I wish we could have a good deal of leisure to talk. I seem, and regret it and hate myself for it, to be able to say many more things I want to in talking than in writing. In a sense I feel in bad enough trouble, yet most of it is of a chronic or central or formulated sort which I more or less assume or accept as inevitable to trying to understand as much as possible and to live, and to being confused enough in motives, hope, and egoism, to keep trying to write it down; and on the whole I'm much more actively interested than I am doleful or desperate, and it is of interest rather than despair that I'd like now to talk, except when I'm actually cracked up. I truly have not any doubt but very strongly the opposite of the balances, some of them clear and positive, and others mysterious, that there are in existence, and it is their interlocking or fusion with "evil" that may be, next to the plain effort to contemplate, the chief "fascination" or binding-into-living; and I'm very much more drawn toward innocence, and the relaxed or abandoned brain, and simplicity and childhood, and the so-called "sub"-human for that matter and "sub"-organic, than I've appeared by the ways I've written; but I'm also interested in finding how qualified, luke-warm at heart, and corrupted so many of the balancers are, and in the idea that nothing does quite so much harm or evil as innocence or guiltlessness which is so innocent it doesn't see the traps and its double or triple meanings. A case in immediate point to me is an article in the *Atlantic Monthly* called *Insight*, about the spirituality of Negroes, in which in all true innocence and sincerity the author, it seems to me, commits one mortal sin after another, against himself, any half decent hope of humanity or humaneness, and those he writes of. And it is of the sort of entanglements he creates *and is un-conscious of* that the best of the participating "world" appears to be made up. I say "it seems to me," knowing I am ignorant and entangled myself, yet to place mine on a level of ignorance with his, I would be simply lying, within the scale in which we can hope or try at all to tell relative truth as against relative falsehood: which is just what he could with equal justice say of anyone he did not in conscience agree with. And yet I feel I could convince him that he is patronizing and that you cannot possibly honor what you patronize.

I had better try to get to work again. I am so confused and tired in one work that I can't even describe the confusion or its causes.

Much love to you,

Rufus.

[*Frenchtown, New Jersey*]
[*December 21, 1938*]

Dear Father:

I tried a couple of weeks back and again just now to answer your letters (I mean particularly on education and on "enough to live on") and I guess I'll have to give it up or at least postpone it: to lay out at all clearly what I believe and why, even as much as I'm clear on myself; and in what ways and why I don't "agree" with you, would take I don't know how long, and I would learn a good deal more anyhow than I know now in the course of trying to. But I can't now. At the most brief possible, though, it is premises I disagree on or am more mixed or qualified on than you. On "education": what I believe you think of as true and good education I think of as such only as a part of a possible education more as a whole; I feel also it can be obstructive or deceptive even to those who are capable of it if it is focused only on its own kinds of intellectual moral centers; that the human race is incurably sick in more entangled ways than has even been suspected, and that focuses of full-education should better be towards fuller realization of this and medical and surgical of mental habits, inherited prejudices, lacks of questioning, etc. etc. and of all the moral ambiguities and woundings of environments which have created present "heredity" and "inheritance" and towards a more general and universal interdependent understanding of what human "health," mental and spiritual and physical, individual and social, would mean.

On "enough to live on"; this depends too on investigations and on education. I'll grant, certainly, plenty are apathetic or brainless, or cynical, or "dishonest" or all these and more, and with plenty of these there would be no use hoping anything, but they are whatever they are through conditions and a world (material and of ideas) which might have been better: this includes all damage done their "moral fibre"; and it would seem to me obvious that it would take a few generations of patience and not of moral blame to clear them off. Too many *causes* are disregarded or thought too lightly of as against a more easy feeling that by and large people are or get what they deserve, or fairly close to it; and the great majority—which lies between John Green and someone entirely "worthless"—is too quickly passed over, as I feel you did, saying in effect, "no doubt some are deprived through misfortune or sickness, or poverty, for which they aren't responsible." These are the same whom cotton landlords describe as shiftless and no good.

Well I can't answer it. Those I appear to be taking sides with—Communists, scientists, etc. take a lot too much for granted in one direction; I feel you take too much for granted in another; others still more; in the middle, a great majority of people keep on suffering under diseases they never asked for and will never understand. Why can't there be a whole method and science of mere skepticism, meaning more faith better grounded? which shall try establishing at least a little more clearly what is taken for granted or overlooked.

I meant mainly, though, only to send you and Mrs. Flye a great deal of love, and my wishes and thoughts that you have a happy Christmas.

Alma and I were married early this month.

Much love to both of you,

Rufus.

[Frenchtown, New Jersey]
[January 13, 1939]

Dear Father:

This will be a very scrapped-up note. I feel too exhausted safely to get straight into my own work and if I were at St. Andrew's would under same circumstances probably stop in and talk just as stupidly as this for a few minutes.

Exhausted because last-night this-morning I managed after two weeks, to break a rhythm of insomnia till 5 A.M. and late waking by kicking myself out of bed paralyzed for lack of sleep. I hope to start getting my reward about 11 tonight; meanwhile if I'm to do any non-demoralizing work or non-work I must go carefully.

Thank you a lot for sending the copy of the *Atlantic Monthly* (I can't say *Atlantic* alone). When it came I quit work a couple of hours looking in and around things you had recommended; as result of this laziness fell into several hours' guilt and work-disintegration; and as result of that, haven't read a word of it since; so I have little ground to comment yet. With basis of *Snobbery on the Left* I have for so long been in intense agreement that I almost regret he wrote it;

I wanted to. I hope I still shall as part of some effort to lay out or suggest the terrific and generally over-looked destructiveness which comes through general ambiguities of meanings of words, actions and concepts, most particularly moral-ideas; and through the narrow-frontedness and lack of self-skepticism of all organized reformers and revolutionists. What hell is worked, for instance, under banner of such words as "love," "loyalty," "honesty," "duty," and their opposites; what are the different meanings of the word "pride"; which seem most destructive of evil and why and how; which may not be; which are not; which are "obligatory," "constructive," and for "good?" I have had and still have some to guard against a form of inverted snobbery in myself, i.e. an innate and automatic respect and humility toward all who are very poor and toward all the unassuming and non-pompous who are old. I'd rather not be without some form of this respect toward them, but it's very dangerous and can easily be false. The *Hired Man* education article I've as yet only started. It looks to be sound criticism from "within-a-system," i.e. by one who believes there could be sufficient good within this system revised. Since I so much doubt this, such criticism seems only secondarily relevant to me. I would believe teaching needs at all times to be noninstitutional; done along the streets, individually as Socrates did it or for that matter as Jesus did; or at very most—organized in the poverty and intensity of the mediaeval beginnings of Universities; that any further organization and acceptance into society suffocated learning how to try to use the mind intensely and independently, i.e. how to become in certain senses a "free" rather than a "bonded" man; this latter being probably the first and maybe the only great obligation of teaching. If or when one has got some of this duty-of-independence, he may then much more safely go about becoming a scholar or whatever he pleases.

Of itself as a poem I like the *Flanders Fields* brought up to date and much in its meaning as against the disgust and disgrace of the selling out. I disagree on some such grounds as this: assuming the soldiers believed most sincerely they were dying to defend and to save almost all hope of good against almost all probability of evil, I think they were tragically deceived (in part by self-deceived men) and could wish they might at length be undeceived and might not protest in terms of the self-deception they died for. I am so confused on war as to be uncertain whether there should or should not have been one over Czechoslovakia and all that was there represented: though that by no means reduces my feeling of the ugliness and perfidy of what did happen. If I had better faith than I do in any of the "democracies" themselves as humane nations I might be clearer in favor of war; as it is, I feel it is a rattlesnake-skunk choice, with the skunk of course considerably less deadly yet not so desirable around the house that I could back him with any favor.

I've been reading Eckermann's *Conversations with Goethe* and by all sorts of straight mental content and psychologically, it is much more than interesting. But I dislike Goethe as a human being and "type" of "artist" and "great man" more than I do almost any man of "genius" except Wagner and in many ways even more, for he represents more. There appear to be two kinds of good artist (at least); the "bishop" type and the "saint" type: I can think of no single overlapping. I not only prefer the "saint" type; I feel the "bishop" type is a traitor to his God and a drag on the Human race. (That is to say nothing of the trouble and confusion the "saints" cause, though.)

A very good movie last night; I believe you would like it, called *A Man to Remember*: the sort of distinctions made in the life of a small-town poor people's doctor and his relation to the world which are inescapable in any religious man in whatever work —and there much more sharply shown than I have seen them before in a movie. The sort of difficult and uncompromising living my friend Walker Evans has been doing the past 12 years as a photographer or "artist" who will not sell out as such of his work or life.

I think (but fear to say optimistically) that I am getting into home stretch on the book. It will be a great relief but also at least as great a sense of loss. I think it will be important to get immediately and hard to work on something else without any rest: otherwise likely to be a let-down which might last for months. I haven't yet learned at all well how to use either time or myself; I'm still nearly helpless to do even passable work unless I have strong feeling, and that exhausts itself and is uneven more than most things. I wouldn't want to lose it but I would wish that in the times between I might write coldly and mentally and steadily as a research scientist does and must.

I'm beginning to teach Alma piano. (She's already a good violinist and musician, so it's easy.) Even this much shows me some funny and tricky things about teaching: that you get a double thing: you actually do "know more" through teaching someone than of your own knowledge; you also have a very dangerous illusion of knowing more than you do. Separating these and holding off and ruining the illusory part would be the trick, or one of them, and difficult. Undoubtedly needs balancing with an equal amount of time being taught by one superior in knowledge to your own: all during the same days. I may try balancing it by learning the violin from Alma.

I made a try lately of writing the book in such language that anyone who can read and is seriously interested can understand it. I felt it was a failure and would take years to learn how to do but became so excited in it I had (and have) a hard time resuming my first method; including a sense of guilt. The lives of these families belong first (if to any one) to people like them and only secondarily to the "educated" such as myself. If I have done this piece of spiritual burglary no matter in what "reverence" and wish for "honesty", the least I can do is to return the property where it belongs, not limit its language to those who can least know what it means. But I can't and should not sacrifice "educated" ideas and interests which the "uneducated" have no chance or reason, yet, to be other than bored by; and until I can keep these yet put them in credible language I guess there's nothing better I can do about it than write as to the "educated." Also in spite of intense convictions I mistrust myself; and if you're going to write what may be poison better write it to adults than to perfectly defenseless children.

At night I'm starting to draw, heads of Alma and copies of postcard American city streets. I would never have known how much even a little of it sharpens your eye and gives you more understanding and affection for even some small part of a human or architectural feature. Also, back with the whole primitive bases of art, when people made effigies that they might have power over the animals they needed for food. I now "possess" and "know" Alma's face and a Brooklyn street in 1938 as if they were a part of me, as much as my hand, the same with one of the tenant houses from memory. I have an idea that in the course of "teaching" either children or adults I'd want that everyone would draw, for a long time, from photographs and from nature first, just as patiently and accurately as they were able; who wanted to learn and "see" the world.

I must quit.

Much love to you and to Mrs. Flye.

Rufus.

Dear Father:

Thank you for both your letters:

I certainly do hope you will come up and will be here a long time. I feel the same wish for long and uninterrupted talks.

It is likely that by July Alma and I will be out of town, about fifty miles, for the summer. If so, though, I hope you will come and stay there all of the time you want to, and anyhow as much of the time as you will: or if you don't, I will anyhow be coming in to see you. If we are here instead, stay with us—there will be plenty of room—but I imagine you might prefer being in New York, more central to seeing people: this is in Brooklyn. There are friends I hope you will want to see and believe you will like. Please do come.

It has been a very bad three months here in New York, full of a good many kinds of anxieties, money, rent and 'psychological' in me. I'm pulled apart between them so that I'm seldom good for much, but they are clearing now I think.

The book is all done but a few pages, which I'm finishing a great deal too slowly. I feel almost nothing about it, pro or con, except a wish to be done with it, a sense of serious gaps in it, and a knowledge that it is 'sincere' and that I made no attempt to take an easy way on it. But so much more is clear or pretty clear in the head that becomes weak and confused when I try to write it.

I want very much to work through the summer but can't yet choose between about 20 things I want to work on, and feel cold and incompetent in each of them . . .

If we were sitting here together I know we could talk differently from this, but differently inclined as I feel, I am fit for nothing trying to write.

I look forward very greatly to seeing you—I hope
you do come up.

Much love to you and to Mrs. Flye

Rufus

Dear Father:

. . . I've been reading a little (very little); finishing
Cocteau (*A Call to Order*), and reading some slowly
in *A Portrait of the Artist*, which makes me ashamed
ever to have thought I'd read it before, and exceedingly suspicious on the whole question of when or
how or how soon to read what: unless there is certain
to be re-reading; and suspicious even then; and suspicious for that matter of my illusion that I am reading it now. I would suspect a chemical rule on
reading as in 'influence,' 'imitation,' and 'plagiarism';
that in reading or being influenced 'successfully' one
does as much work as the authors did originally. Leaving however, very little time for writing, and not quite
true. But I am sick in myself and others of the illusion of reading which comes of somewhat intelligently skimming a great work, being somewhat
excited by it, and thinking from that that you 'know'
or 'understand' it. Exact analogy to those who meet at
receptions and thenceforth claim to know such men,
calling them perhaps by their private nicknames. I
could be glad not to dare to use the name Shakespeare
or Joyce or Beethoven, etc. etc., ever again, or only
in most exceedingly qualified contexts.

It may be I will work now on editing and organiz-
ing (selecting) a collection of letters: but more likely
not; for the idea is the mutual property of three, and
I doubt *Harpers* will advance sufficient to three. If it
should go through, and if places and identities (prob-

ably even names of editors) are disguised, would you be willing if letters of yours should be used? Subject even so, needless to say, to discretion of privacy on this matter and that; but would you? I put together 35 or 40 letters yesterday, into a binding, organized, and they did look good to me.

You might not see it, so I would want specifically to recommend the movie of *Good Bye, Mr. Chips*; I think possibly you'd like it a good deal. I had just the same feeling of it as of the book; definite liking and definitely touched or even moved; mixed with suspicion, slight resentment of self and author at being moved by suspect material; and considerable basic disagreement with almost the whole 'philosophic' substance of it; in fact, a dislike of it much more intense than I had the puritanism to let myself feel, because that would spoil a nice warm bath of sentimental enjoyment. Because of lack of money, I am these days much more temperate than I want to feel or be. Back to *Chips* as example of something: something of what it is talking of I consider to be sacred territory. In proportion to sacredness of territory one needs to be merciless of mishandling (no matter how sincere) and merciless towards the sincerely part-good which can almost always be moving and inspire generosity toward its weakness. In certain respects this mercilessness is non- or anti-Christian. It is absolutely required however of a 'good artist,' meaning a 'pure' 'heart,' meaning a 'moral' 'man.' I am personally confused on this and by my own definition of what ought to be, am frequently a bad artist, impure of heart, and an immoral man. So my tentative statement of right is a statement mainly of desire, so far as I am concerned. Seeing it in another, though, I unqualifiedly respect it. He is being the morally hardest thing I can think of: cruel toward sincerity in the name of relative truth.

No other movies (though you might like *On Bor-*

rowed Time; I did, somewhat as I liked Mr. Chips). Did you ever see *Maedchen in Uniform* or do you know of it? I wish you could see it. A hard old-fashioned Prussian-type girls' school; one good, young, teacher; the best adolescent children who have ever been in movies (or written of, as far as I know); and of these one in particular singled out, gentle and scarcely emerged; who falls desperately in love with the good teacher and through a scandal arising of this, attempts suicide. In her attempt the Prussian-symbol in education (the head-mistress) is convinced of her wrong and is withered. There are movies which by power, or technique, or theory of subject, and handling, I think are greater, but none I could like much better. I hope you will see it some time if you haven't.

Yesterday was Alma's birthday. Emma* was down. We had a cake and a number of things which aren't made as pretty or as well for anyone else as for Woolworth's; Chinese straw fans, an artificial flower, cheap white net gloves.

Going to town now; mail this. It was wonderful to see you. Next time has got to be sooner; and I should think that will be possible.

Rufus

* Emma Agee Ling, Jim's sister.

Dear Father:

This won't or shouldn't be much of a letter, but knowing I must be at work and that I am poorer in answerings in ratio to length of time deferred, I do want to do a little, no matter how cheap, short and dead-minded it is. Above all please forgive the deadness, for my only way through is to try to ignore it myself—or rather flatly recognize it and do nothing about it. Thank you a great deal for your letters and for all clippings . . .

The offending words or phrases you write of: on the whole question I am not by any means fully sure of myself but I realize I must quite essentially disagree with you on these. Though many of my agreements could seem almost identical. I think for instance I dislike most levels of foulmouthedness quite as intensely as you do. One difference is, I feel it is possible to be quite as foul mouthed using a euphemism or an aseptic or so called scientific word as the word in general vulgar or forbidden use. My hatred is not of the words any more than of the acts; it is of those who misuse them, and of the ways they are misused. But again: I feel no word can be quite as dirty as the word sexual intercourse where it is used wrongly. It is not a restoration of words of themselves I care for but a restoration of attitudes or "philosophy" of which all words are gruesomely accurate betrayals. I have been and am still guilty of a variable and at times very coarse taste or judgment, but I can't remember having groogled or leered or smirked since I was in the cheap-irony stage at about fifteen. I feel just as chary and as self-suspicious of my over-frequent use in writing of the name of God or of William Blake. Well, I'll shut up.

Of J. T. Adams writing on children my feelings are mixed, between some agreement and surprise and a still undiluted dislike of the man himself or rather of his kind; so that some of my feeling is "What *right* have you to any such attitude or liking?" As I would feel if he praised *Ulysses* or put in a favorable word for God. If I were a beautiful child I'd want my choice of whose eyes were on me. I agree with Tate except in certain respects: (a) I think human beings might do exceedingly well to learn from animals and hope to come half-way up to them, rather than exert themselves in distinguishing themselves from them; (b) much 'useless' knowledge seems to me as choking and paralyzing as most of the 'useful' knowledge. But I know in what terms he is meaning 'useful' and 'useless' and I certainly agree.

I'm sorry to be writing by hand. The noise of a typewriter would unbalance what little brain I have right now.

I'm glad you'll be willing if the Letters book comes through. It won't at present, though. I don't dare specify what I'm starting to write. I feel too insecure in it even as I am. I can say this much, though. I'm beginning a thing which I mistrust; and am going under contract for it (which I abominate) and am thereby deferring work I would prefer to do; because it is the only way I can get money to live and do anything of work I can call my own. I therefore feel cold, sick, vindictive, powerless and guilty against the world and between the wish to take vengeance on myself and on *Harpers* and 'the world,' and the wish to do the best I can, and feelings of hopeless coldness and incompetence, I can't even feel much anger, far less anything better. This may change. I hope it does, for I am drawing in to a dead point. I'd be very glad of a person I could trust (and afford) to do mental surgery on me, and far more glad to grow up and need no such pother. Meanwhile I am thirty and have missed irretrievably all the trains I should have caught.

Much love to you.

R.

Don't feel concern or pain over this last. It's only one of several 'states of mind' and if I ever live it must be by having learned to take care of myself.

My dear friend:

I hope you will forgive how long it has been since I have written. In short pieces of open time I have started several letters to you—they were interrupted and never finished. This is no full answer either— however a superficial one—but send you my love, and my love to Mrs. Flye—my loving thought and esteem and remembrance of both of you. I think of you as you both, and mother, and father have been through midnight mass and Christmas and through today and sleeping now and I feel my own strenuousness and callowness and ignobility and my heart goes out to you. I think I probably reach out toward you all and towards the Catholic faith as towards parents and wisdom and peace and my childhood. That may be a weak and panicked thing to do but that may not be a bad idea of itself. I care a great deal to try to understand and approach and receive the center of the storm but there is such a thing too as learning enough when you're half drowned to come in out of the rain. I wish I might be seeing you and that we might talk an unlimited length of time. I wish also I had the stamina and courage to write poetry.

It could have been so much worse for Mrs. Flye.* My gratefulness it wasn't is even more than my feeling of the awful ugliness that anything should have happened to her. My dear, and forgive me for calling

* She had been injured, though not too seriously, in an automobile accident.

you so, I hope you are much better and will be entirely well now.

Good night, and God bless and keep you both.

Rufus

Dear Father:

It will be only a note again and long past due. I feel that in my long failures to write and to return letters you enclosed I have hurt you, and I don't wonder, but I do dread lest you think it is lack of love for you or of wish to communicate. It isn't. Between jobs, occasional attempts to write of my own, personal worries, and a smattering of ill organized social life, I am so generally drowned I am incapable of time or clarity of mind. I have a really dangerous and to me terrifying lack not only of discipline of thought and conduct but of any hold to take towards learning discipline—this along with tendency to melancholia, a habit of thinking emotionally, and its alternate *accidia* (all these are doubtless interactive) makes a fair amount of my living numb and a certain amount of it hell.

I am in (just now) a fairly common state; I feel very much like talking, by mouth; but have nothing to put on paper. So it will be a bald sort of note.

On the clipping you sent of Lippmann on the Youth Congress I feel on some points agreement with him but in the main simply fairly intense disagreement both with him and with those he attacks. I must say I prefer their anger to the smug safeplaying of most people their age (I am thinking of many Harvard students), yet their particular type of anger and actions has always nauseated me—as much as any one thing kept me out of the Communist party when I was nearest to joining it. But so far as government

– 113 –

politics, and a number of other things are concerned I am much more interested in what is wrong than in what is half-heartedly right. There are ideas, or ideals, I think I would die for (if necessary) but none as they are polluted in the hands of governors. I know we live here under certain advantages not obtainable in Germany or Russia, but since when should a people plume itself on obvious virtue without which one is unfit to live—particularly when even that virtue is poisoned and betrayed, less frequently but no less effectively— to say nothing of a thousand vices. I prefer a little free speech to no free speech at all; but how many have free speech or the chance for the mind for it; and is not free speech here as elsewhere clamped down on in ratio of its freedom and danger?

I am talking much too thin here and I will stop. My main feeling is simply that there is little that I will render to Caesar beyond taking care at intersections; because I feel that what is the legal property of Caesar is the actual property of God. I certainly have lost a great deal in faith, hope, and optimism in a few years —I have little if any hope left that the cancer will ever be even slightly alleviated, far less cured; but rather than simply moderating my "political affiliations" the result (so far) is to drive me towards art, psychology and religion. If I weren't an anarchist I would probably be a left-wing conservative—though I write even the words with superstitious dread. I never in all my life want to feel respect for a half-good.

Our child* will be born within a short time now,— a week or two. On that I feel such complications of hope, fear, joy, sorrow, life, death, foreboding, interest, and a dozen other true emotions on which the copyright has expired, that I am not qualified to try to touch them now. On the whole, though, I can

* Joel Agee.

notice that whereas I am much moved and excited by Ideas—related with general existence and with art—in my own personal living and performance itself I am a far from sanguine person. I don't know whether "cure" is possible or even advisable—I do suspect, though, that unless I learn some new holds or disciplines, I shall sooner or later break my heart or mind or both, without ever having done one thing I most wanted to and should have.

I must stop and get back to work. I hope you are well, and I send much love to you and to Mrs. Flye.

Rufus.

[New York City]
Sept. 21, 1941

Dear Father:

I had hoped to write at real length, but I expect I won't for two reasons. I am very tired; and I want to send you a letter, rather than begin a serial.

You have sent many things, in your letters themselves, and photographs and enclosures, which I would like to write of at leisure and, I hope, will; it is just what I lack the stamina to do now. So I want to write, as I would talk if we could, only of the few most urgent things you have written of—all to do with me: general health, diet, sleep, the possibilities of marriage, of psychiatry, of a child.

On all you write of health, diet, sleep, schedule, general discipline, I substantially, and as far as that goes passionately agree, and am already making a little headway. By 'as far as that goes' I mean something rather serious, though: that if I can work out a broadly simple and quiet way of using myself and keeping myself in good order, there is nothing I more desire or more acutely realize the need of. But that as that approaches *intricacy* of diet or schedule or a sense of too sedulous an economy towards, or taking care of, myself, it destroys its own ends. Nothing makes me more frantic than too careful a manner-of-speaking of always being sure to wear my rubbers. That of course is at the root of my almost total lack of sense and discipline.

But I don't think it likely that I'll overdo self-discipline—so actually, I agree with you, and am already—not with more than small success yet—at work on it.

Psychiatry, and for that matter psychoanalysis still more, interest me intensely; but except for general talk with them—which I would like—I feel reluctant to use either except in really desperate need. I don't yet feel in desperate need, and suspect in fact that I'll probably pull out of this under my own power. Yet I realize that I have an enormously strong drive, on a universally broad front, toward self-destruction; and that I know little if anything about its sources or control. There is much I might learn and be freed from that causes me and others great pain, frustration and defeat, and I expect that sooner or later I will have to seek their help. But I would somewhere near as soon die (or enter a narcotic world) as undergo full psychoanalysis. I don't trust anyone on earth that much; and I see in every psychoanalyzed face a look of deep spiritual humiliation or defeat; to which I prefer at least a painful degree of spiritual pain and sickness. The look of "I am a man who finally could not call his soul his own, but yielded it to another . . ."

R.

Dear Father:

It's a pleasure not only to hear from you but for once to have a little time immediately, to answer in.

Desultory conversation. No harm in that though, I suppose, if only it isn't too dull to read.

Odd juxtapositions—the way two little grains of the same distant period will suddenly and for no traceable reason turn up within a few hours of each other, like running a series on the same number in roulette. And what they do to you. The immediate example is that I spent a fair part of the afternoon looking at a book of photographs by Cecil Beaton. I've always rather scorned him—today I rather respected him, seeing 500 photographs together. They're perfection for the apex—late 20's maybe—of post-war upper-class-arty England: bisexual, dandyish, corrupt, semi-classicist with a strong romantic undertaint, melancholic, and frivolous. Beauties, whores, entertainments, ballet, first-class second-class artists, wilful and ultra-sophisticated "bad taste." Shameful against pure and deep work like Walker's but historically and sentimentally full of meaning and a kind of beauty. It brought all of that and all of my tendencies in that direction sharply awake. When I came home (as I laughingly call it) and upstairs, people are for the first time playing Façade, poems by Edith Sitwell spoken to music by Wm. Walton—the essence of that same period—which I knew by heart ten years ago and have scarcely heard or thought of for five. I could add, for that matter, a related thing: seeing 4 short movies yesterday, made in Paris in the early to middle 20's and much more sympathetic to me than anything which has been done since, outside Eisenstein, Dovchenko, and some things in my own head. That in turn brought back with great power the regret I have that I didn't spend several years in Paris instead of several years at Harvard and writing on *Fortune*. Excepting my doubt that my mind was—or is—really fit for it. I have a funny, very middle-class, and in a bad sense of the word, Christian mind, and a very clouded sensibility. To use my mind cleanly is as intense but also as rare and brief a desire to me as occasional returns of religiousness. Good minds, like good souls, don't have to make that elementary, childish sort of resolution.

The physiognomy question really interests me by its variety and unreliability. As unreliable as several persons' reading of a poem. You wrote on the back of my picture: "Hope you like this. I do. It makes me want to smile back and think 'What pleasant things there are in life,' " "Clinically," which is a tag I dislike, this interests me: When I first saw the picture—before I saw the writing—I (a) thought I was someone else, and disliked him rather, and (b) recognized myself and was shocked, seeing in the face complacency, coarseness, a kind of intelligence which overestimated itself, and a kind of duplicity which interested me but about which I was unable to reach any clear analysis. Then I read what you had written and felt still worse: love for you and for your kindness and tolerance or innocence of my evil; and shame that I had, intentionally or not, thus deceived you. Then I began to feel precisely as you did about the picture, and even with some thoroughness to like myself. My present feeling is an amalgam of all of these. Through laziness, certainly, and stupidity or lack of method which I might better recognize if I were less lazy, I cannot (don't) get this into analysis more detailed than vague remarks about the corners of my mouth, and the set of my eyes—far less do I make any headway about my changed feeling from self-distaste to self-affection. So I'm not advancing the science of Physiognomy. But as an undigested note, I think it's of some interest.

I could add to it.

The picture of Mr. W.—before I saw his name on the back—was a peculiarly charming study of an elderly, middle-class, conservative, semi-cultivated, man—of moderate property—an almost darling quality of gentle satire about it. Considerably out-of-character with most that I know of Mr. W. After seeing his name (I was amazed, and slightly embarrassed) I tried to reconcile—and so nearly succeeded that my first image is far removed, like a little trick or toy rather than a reality or even a felt illusion.

And Mia. With all people I love, I am liable to melt, and move too near to see them straight. So that I saw in her a peculiarly lordly air of deep sadness first not through my own eyes but through Walker's. Both these photographs record it, and make it clearer to me than I almost ever personally see it. I suppose— one half-good piece of analysis for a change—that this demonstrates the distance between the coolness and truth of any camera's or any classical human eye and that sludginess of my own; and that by enough study and meditation I could cleanse my own . . .

A hard week. Work, finding an apartment, moving, and called to show whether I qualify for jury duty. Between all these I am sure I can't yet see Payson Loomis. But I want to. And I have long felt I wanted to talk with men in other fields, particularly scientific, technical and trained-philosophic. I begin to feel, as I may have mentioned, very ill-educated. A Viennese friend of Mia's is interesting me much to talk with. His fields are related esthetics, music, art, architecture —but it is his very sharp use of his mind that most interests me . . .

What you write of the book* needless to say is good to hear to the point of shaming me—for it is a sinful book at least in all degrees of "falling short of

---

* *Let Us Now Praise Famous Men* had just been published.

the mark" and I think in more corrupt ways as well. Mrs. Flye's feeling for it I feel even better about, for I feel her judgment is at depths and levels I only apprehend, and perhaps most greatly respect of any level I can apprehend . . .

Showed a number of your photographs to Helen, who much likes the feeling and atmosphere of them. I saw the first batch of her Mexican prints and am much excited by the best of them. A completely magical set, of very little girls playing: what ballet can never get to.

I must stop and get to work. Much love to you and to Mrs. Flye.

R.

[New York City]
[June 14, 1943]

Dear Father:

I wrote you but can't remember whether I mailed it. The main news is brief and there is nothing much else besides. I got back here to find I had been reclassified 3-A (not immediately draftable); but now have just been reclassified 1-A (for immediate induction). The Board tells me that means induction either in July or August. So presumably (I can never count on anything they say) I'll be around for a while, while you're here, anyway. I would be glad enough, I feel just now, to have a nervous breakdown if I could arrange it, but my constitution, as far as I can gauge it, is of the particular, amphibious sort which will pass such tests without much reducing the final quota of misery to me. The only positive feeling I have for being in it is really a negative one—that in one single respect it is not happy to be out of a thing in which so many are suffering. But that is as much as I can conceivably feel in its favor . . .

If I don't see you all that I might during the time we are both here, I hope you'll forgive and understand it . . . Particularly with the draft very near, I want, if I can, to do some writing. The pressures of work are such even now that I am in a daily nerve-ending frustration. So I will have to do my best to square off and guard some evenings. But I only hope that in trying to do so, I will not seem to you not to want to see you, and much more than I manage to, or in fact of course I do very much want to. Very likely you do understand this perfectly; my difficulty is, I am and have always been obsessed with the doubt, all around, that such things are understood. Will you give my love to Mrs. Flye. And to you, always.

Rufus

[New York City]
[October 30, 1943]

Dear Father:

Very briefly—and thank you for both letters.

I had heard elsewhere that Lowell* was sentenced and jailed. I am very glad to find where, and how to reach him and his wife, for (unless on more careful thought I feel he might prefer otherwise) I want to write, and if possible see him; and his wife if she wants or needs friends and I am apposite.

In Charles' letter, one or two points. I realize (I think well) how limited his time is, and how much it means to him to use it well. But in his comment on *War and Peace* "my time was well spent" seemed also to have a different tone, which he would greatly gain by learning different about. I may be exaggerating what in my own case was only spontaneous rather

---

* Robert Lowell, as a conscientious objector.

than very conscious, but wondered whether there may not be there (in keeping thoroughly with his unusually grave, methodical and clear mind) a basicall mistaken, limited, puritanical conception of wh. reading, knowledge, living, enjoyment, is for. So much is bound to be lost if it is too carefully coveted. I would imagine he either knows this or would quietly realize it if it were well and sympathetically (a pleonasm) presented. I hope you will.

On our plans for post-war and on Russia, I should either write hours or not at all. I expect the worst of us and of the English; something so little better in most respects (if we get our way) than Hitler would bring, that the death of a single man is a disgrace between the two. I would expect very little good of Russia (or of Chiang Kai-shek even less), but hope at best there will be balance between these powers, forced by the final chance outcome of the war. And that I have little hope for.

I am doing movies again,* rather than books, but want to read the Roussy de Sales.

What, so far, is happening this year? I'm eager to hear more—and hope to write at more length soon.

Much love,

Jim

* For *Time*. See *Agee on Film*, Vol. I (McDowell, Obolensky, 1958).

Dear Father:

I'm very sorry not to have returned David's letter
long before this. It got mixed up in a change of coats,
then in my work, then in my guilt, which can neatly
prevent my doing just what would relieve it. Much
the same is why I've for so long failed to write at
least a line.

You wonder whether other people share your distaste for using the word *Jap*. I do, from the bottom
of my liver. Also *Nip, Nippon, Sub* (even *U-Boat*
bothers me though I sometimes use it), and *war effort*.
I am sure I could think of more, if I could think at all.
Yes, *Jerry*—at least when an American uses it; even
if I were an Englishman I don't think I'd want to.
And *Reds*. And *Muscovites*. And *Russ*. And *Blitz*
(though it's a good word). People who use such
words would also talk of their tummy.

Late at night I've been doing some reading—which
I shamefully lack the energy to do more than list.
Stendhal's *The Red and the Black; The Good Soldier
Schweik* by Jaroslav Hasek; and a book analyzing
Blake's poems and minor prophecies. The one I recommend 97 per cent to you is Schweik, which might
be St. Andrew's transplanted to the Austro-Hungarian
Army—the funniest and sorest satire on bureaucrats,
authoritarians, scientists and other poops that I have
ever read. Also a very good book on E. M. Forster by
Lionel Trilling, who writes very finely about the naive
liberal assumption that the world is redeemable and
divisible in terms of sheep and goats, who are terribly
offended by the world when it doesn't play ball that
way, and who above all are baffled by a novelist
(Forster) so wicked as to make comedy of them and
of the world and to be a liberal himself. He quotes
Stendhal as observing that Gaiety is the sign of the
intelligent man—a statement which ought to be writ-

ten across practically every "intelligent" forehead I know of.

The Stendhal is wonderful. I've never seen more beautiful narration of cross-purpose between people, intricate mutual and self-deceptions, the evil that can grow out of a good impulse, the good that can grow out of an evil one.

I've been specially wishing I could see you since borrowing from Jimmy Stern two books of poems by John Betjeman (Welsh-English, Jimmy says) called *Continual Dew* and *Old Lights for New Channels*. I'll enclose some quotes, but I'm not sure they're enough to show why I think you'd like him so much. I'll quote from Betjeman's preface: "The suburbs, thanks to *Punch*, which caters for them, are now considered 'funny'. Some people still think Victorian industrial scenery is only fit for invective. Churches are always 'funny' when they are written about by a devotional writer. Gaslight is funny. Post Street is funny, all sorts of places and things are funny if only the funny writers are funny about them. I love suburbs and gaslights and Post Street and Gothic Revival churches, provincial towns and garden cities. They are, many of them, part of my bodyguard. From them I try to create an atmosphere which will be remembered by those who have had a similar bodyguard, when England is all council houses and truck roads and steel and glass factory blocks in the New Europe after the war." They are as pure English as anything I know.

Well, I'm tired already, and still want to copy some for you. So I'll stop.

Goodnight and love to you—and thank you especially, Father, for your New Year's letter.

Rufus

Dear Father:

One way to write a letter since I fail by all other means: it is ten to seven; I am due for an appointment at 7; I will turn on the tap and let it run for 8 minutes and send the result whatever it may be. Thank you for your letter and for the several others I so regret failing to answer. It has been rather a heavy fall and winter. Trip to Hollywood; upon return Emma was painfully sick in hospital and I spent nearly all evenings with her and afterwards with Don; by the time she was out, Alma and Joel had arrived; they left again for Mexico about 10 days ago; I have managed to do very little work of my own and though I feel some hope of doing so for the first time in months, having a little prospect of free time, I now face my own hopeless inefficiency with time and lack of discipline and somewhat obscurer type of work-blockage; I suppose the next 6 weeks or so will show me something, one way or the other. I am glad you are likely to be coming up for the summer. When my own vacation will be, spring or summer or fall, I can't yet be sure, but in any event I will surely be in town most of the time you are here.

I begin to want to write a weekly column for some newspaper or magazine—very miscellaneous but in general, detailed topical analysis of the very swift and sinister decline and perversion of all that might be meant by individualism, a sense of evil, a sense of tragedy, a sense of moral vigilance or discrimination; the perversion of virtually all nominal rationalism to the most irrational sort of uses and ends; the fear of the so-called irrational, the mock-revival of mock-religion; and well, etc. etc. Whatever dignified thing may ever have been meant by "liberalism", such a thing as a true "liberal" hardly exists any more, one no longer knows one's friends from one's enemies. I lately heard several highly intelligent people talk about the courtroom mobbing of Caretta in a way which was an exact parallel of the condoning of a lynching.

My time is up. I'm afraid I've not made myself at all clear. But the idea would be to work as hard against the grain as possible in a would-be liberal paper, for that sort of reader. It includes anything between the bringing-up of children and an analysis of advertising copy and the several prevalent attitudes about "war criminals". Well, goodbye for the moment and much love to you and to Mrs. Flye.

Jim.

[New York City]
[March 29, 1945]
Early Maundy Thursday

Dear Father:

Christ is risen. I'm sorry I can't write it to you in Greek. Without religion in a sense I knew, and that could be called religion, I am aware of Holy Week, and trying to keep it, in a way I have not in a long time. I am each year aware of it, sharply, but not for a long time enough that I have felt I had any business doing anything about it. It seems unlikely that I will ever become fully religious or a communicant again. But I hope I need not tell you, and feel sure you will not scorn, how grateful I am for such religious feelings as I do have. This is all a mess, and better left unwritten or else much more carefully said, but I am too tired either to write it well or to keep off it, since it is on my mind, and you are the person I would most like to talk to.

Forgive the previousness of my salutation. I have as much a sense of the end as of the Passion, and wrote it as I would wish you a happy Easter, knowing it will reach you on Monday or so.

I have to doubt so much that at the same time I trust: thoughts and realizations mixed with personal and historic memories and projections so fill me with tears, and with faith and certainty, that it seems incredible to me not to be a Christian and a Catholic in the simplest and strictest senses of the words. But I am at once grateful for the emotions and doubtful of them.

Thank you for the Rebecca West line—a very good one—and for the Kipling poem, which I have always liked a lot. Do you know Eliot's selections from Kipling and his essay on him? I think you'd like both. The book most on my mind now is *The Final Struggle* —diaries—by Tolstoy and his wife, recording the last year of his life. If it is in Sewanee, I hope you'll read it. If not, I have it here. I can think of very few books that are anything like really heart-breaking, and it's one of them.

I'm grateful you like the idea of the column. I'm still doubtful I could keep it up, or make it good enough. I would think self-attack and self-doubt to be very proper parts of such a column; but if they turned out to occupy 90 per cent of the space, they belong in a journal, not journalism. I am going to try a few weeks specific practice, and see how it goes and whether I can carry it with the other work. Much as such things attract me, I'm leery of taking them on when even now I do so little about the work I most wish personally to do. Some day I'll know how young it was to be 35. But right now it is a terrifying age.

I'll have to stop, but I'll write before long again. It is good to hear from you.

Jim

One night Mia and I played a game, of writing verses on the first word we turned to in a book

(*Grimm's Fairy Tales*). I enclose a couple of samples, with very little good in them, but a little.

(on the word *asleep*)

Asleep, perfected, you would never believe
Harm of a one of them. That stirring hand,
That leg, might clasp, endear, be brought across
An enemy, as gently as a wife.
How God must grieve,
Watching in all this shadow land
The flinching vigil candles of this countless loss
In night's nave each a life:
Who groans, smiles, murmurs, quiets; then on the
  horn
Transpierced, assembles upward, and reborn,
By all that skill and bravery crowns him with
Works, while he wakes, to put himself to death.

(on the word *kingdom*)

In that kingdom no one cries.
No one doubts, for no one lies.
No son ever dreads his mother,
Nor no brother envies brother.

Families, there like nearby trees
Spring and shelter, and the bees
Groan among the cloudy flowers;
Angels, each a soul devours.

There continually the smile
Of the heart that knows no guile.
There, untroubled, people greet
Death like an old friend in the street.

Dear Father:

Thank you for your letter. This is another spare-moment reply. I'm in a bad temper (heat, rush, behind on NATION work, still worse behind on work of my own, hopelessness of ever getting free time, hopelessness of ever using it well if I do) of which I must warn you; I hope I won't take any of it out on you or in this note. I'm partly worried about that because the main thing that pricks up my ears, or the hair along my back, in your letter, as probably you can imagine, is what you say of the anti-discrimination legislation. The things you object to, I object to also; I intensely dislike coercion of that or any other kind, and it is all a part of a much larger texture of coercions which are becoming more and more assured as necessary or anyhow as inevitable. But with at least equal intensity I dislike the forms of discrimination which this kind of legislation is trying to combat. There are very few ways of combatting it, and on the whole I am afraid they are worse than useless; but such as the ways are, and poor as they are, I am for them. The surprising part about them, too, is that they seem to work. In the Army, in those few instances where Whites and Negroes have really been flung together rather than just torturingly and stupidly rubbed together, the difficulties which were expected to make their good functioning virtually impossible, were dissolved quite quickly. In subways here, and at civil service desks, Negroes are much used—used enough that it is for that matter a little silly and selfconscious—but it is working well; people accept without strain or affectation what many of them must have supposed in absence of the fact would be difficult or impossible to accept. A thing I feel you overlook in your objection to it is the general though not universal fact that people are, through their race or religion (or sex) discriminated against not just in those ways alone but economically; and very severely in that respect. The whole complex of those preferences and prejudices the right to whose indulgence you are defending, works to help keep Negroes (for instance) by the millions, impoverished, and in the case of Jews, where it is economically much more jagged, works towards keeping them clannish, interdependent and predatory. That seems very important to me. But even if it weren't; if nobody or group suffered economically through it; I would object just as strongly. One can do nothing in the long run to force or persuade a Jew-hater to like Jews or to cease generalizing (which is more to the point); but I feel no more like defending him through the law than I do like making laws to protect those who like to seduce little girls with candybars.

Each of us really is talking about what we regard as a "right." You feel strongly about the right of a man to hire or not hire whom he pleases. So do I. But I also feel that any human being has the right not to be discriminated against in order to indulge somebody's right to hate, for instance, Jews or Negroes. I feel it the more strongly because I don't regard that right to hate as a right at all but as a deadly wrong. That the hatred exists does not justify its existence, any more than the existence in each or most of us of cruelty or vengefulness justifies cruelty or vengefulness. I realize that the emotional ramifications and depths behind this kind of dislike or fear are all but infinite and are far beyond the personal reach or responsibility of most who feel it (Whites in the South about Negroes I think of); and that such legislation is headed for trouble, as well as for the traduction of certain kinds of rights. Well it may be of minor importance or difference, but I would rather see change and trouble arise as little bloodily and brutally as possible; and though such methods as this will certainly bring about some, I am sure that infinitely worse will come if they are not used. When you watch it in its potentialities it is of course fully tragic and hopeless; and the temptation is strong to prefer the relative tranquility of the present or past. But nothing on earth is going to stop the change; just as nothing on earth is going to bring it through to any good. And the question between which is right, or more greatly right, seems very little question at all if any. (I mean that one seems far more greatly right.) . . .

R.

[New York City]
[May 21, 1945]
Dear Father:

Another quick-one. I'm in no shape or leisure to discuss the race business, etc., very sensibly—far less the more difficult one of "right." I think I feel as I think you do, that the practical facts and the practical possible outcome are both hopeless; but that of course doesn't prevent attitudes, beliefs, hopes, efforts, relative yet real possible gains and losses, and the effort to evaluate all of these.

About "right" I have a feeling the word and concept is confused (but understandably so) with the word "right," meaning just, or morally intact or unquestionable, and with the concept of right or rightness. That all human beings are in all most essential ways equal—i.e. Human, alive, for not long, and compounded of a great and in many ways inextricable mixture of elements and tendencies more or less possible to call good, and evil; and that all human beings are essentially equal in their mortal need; and that they all bear, God knows in various and unequal degrees, the same equality in the potentiality of each, or its self-defeat, or its frustration from outside;—this is poorly expressed and inaccurate, but I would feel or believe that it is true. It seems at the basis of Christian understanding and quite aside from that, elementary to human understanding; a basis of equality which none of the million inequalities of temperament or endowment, all of which should be recognized, can touch. If this is true, then I believe that which supports it to be "right," and that which opposes it to be "wrong." And so by shift I feel or believe rather that every man has the "right" to this recognition, both abstractly and concretely, and that those who oppose or frustrate this right are in the wrong. It seems in other words a "rightness" so fundamental that the question of it as a legal or moral or social "right" "ought" to be irrelevant, and exists and is abused or perverted purely because the fundamental, elementary "rightness" of it is so ill-recognized and so often violated. It is because the violations are so massive and so extraordinarily crude, that the efforts to rectify it are in their turn, and perhaps they have to be, so crude in their own way. In the exacerbation of both sides of the argument, all or most possible good and truthfulness is lost or, still worse, misused; the maniacal rage of the man who is obsessed by his "rights," or the rights of others (say an egalitarian Negro); the equally maniacal reactions of, say, the Southern white employer whose own "rights" are threatened. Neither, at that stage, is capable of the magnanimity, both rational and spiritual, which is the essence of the idea of equality; but I feel no doubt which idea is the more magnanimous; and the exceedingly magnanimous ideas developed, at the best, out of the idea of noblesse oblige compare unfavorably, even so, because I do, here, come to an absolute conviction: that their premises are false, and that those of the kind of basic equality I'm speaking of are true. In other words it is at that point that I become a bigot; and in the most characteristic way of bigots, for on that point I cannot conceive that any other point of view is possibly right.

That the principles of equality have been abused and will be still worse abused, I realize; but without particular surprise; I feel the effort is endless; and the abuse of the privileges of equality seems to me precisely the same thing to contest as the frustration of equality in the first place. Only the focus naturally does shift. Among egalitarians my contest is with those who misconceive or abuse (and so frustrate) the idea; Among anti-egalitarians my contest is with their mere opposition. Without understanding nearly enough about it I nevertheless get the impression I understand more about the attitudes of both sides and the numerous types and levels of both sides, in the Negro-White business, than anyone else I happen to know; through this and a sense of monstrous things ahead I often feel a strong pull, even obligation, towards trying to act as a mediator, moderator and mutual explainer in the battle; but I am immobilized several ways there too: understanding so little and knowing it; the still stronger desire and sense of obligation towards trying to make works of art; the knowledge of the chemical inevitability of the function and fate of mediators and of their hopeless, terrible uselessness; the certainty of the overall uselessness of all that will transpire.

I must stop; late for supper. I am just finishing reading *Black Boy*, by Richard Wright. If a copy is convenient, I very highly recommend it.

Much love to you.

Rufus

Dear Father:

Thanks very much for your three letters. I'm very sorry I have only the last one here, and can't answer with more pertinence. Thanks for telling me of Allen Tate's coming to New York. I'll call him in my first likely breathing-spell, which ought to be about the end of the week. I'll do this with some embarrassment (relieved by hearing he hopes he may see me) because for several weeks now I should have replied to his invitation to review a book about movies, for the *Sewanee Review*. By the way, judging by the summer issue, the only one I've seen, he is making a good magazine of it. Also, by the way, my hair stood on end both with interest and at times intense disagreement (on many points in this you and I couldn't agree), reading Donald Davidson's article about some aspects of the so-called Negro Problem. I do wholly agree with him (and I imagine you) on one point: that infinitely more harm than good will come of the pro-Negro Federal legislation.

I'm glad you are through the Operation and I very much hope you are through it well, without lasting or too severe discomfort (and glad that you got back On Time.) I'm afraid, by a sort of quietness in your references to it, that you're not very comfortable or well yet. I can agree with your fortitude and fatalism if this is so, and admire them too, but they don't prevent any strong sympathy and regret, nor my concern, that you take care not to let Stoicism cause you the slightest avoidable or unnecessary discomfort. (I imagine that could possibly trap and deceive you into trouble, somewhat as Whittaker Chambers has done for himself out of similar plus far more intricate and neurotic reasons. Whittaker, by the way, had a second bad set of scares with his heart, and has changed his job for a much quieter one.) From now on, for at least 6 months and I hope permanently, he will review books for *Time* from his farm, coming to town only about once a month.

I too have changed ½ my job—as temporary, 2 to 3 months' experiment. No more movie reviews for *Time* (though I'll continue for the *Nation*); but "roving" i.e. free-lance through all parts of the magazine, doing whatever miscellaneous pieces seem best for me to be used on. My two great doubts of the job are 1) causing resentment and insecurity among writers whose articles I take away, troublesome both to me and to them and to the managing editor and the whole working climate of the place; 2) that I'll be working harder than on movies, thus reducing seriously my spare time for my own work. If this or these guesses turn out so, I have the promise of my old job back. So I am enjoying the change and the whole experiment a good deal. My first job,* though, almost wholly eliminates spare time, and interests me as much as any piece of personal writing I could possibly be doing: a general article not more than 1500 words long, on Europe this Fall: special emphasis on the coming of winter, the likelihood of massive starvation, the certainty of enormous suffering, the absolute inadequacy of planned or possible relief, from anywhere, above all this country, which alone has enough food (and possibly enough fuel) to guarantee that none of that physical suffering would be necessary. That adequate relief can be shown to be impossible on its present or any Provisional basis (laws, etc.); possible only on a basis of absolute sympathy and generosity. For the practical-minded or outright ungenerous, there are the certain political consequences of the failure: an ineradicable hatred of this country (justified and rational or not) and a tremendous gravitation towards totalitarianism. We write at least the

---

* "Europe: Autumn Story," *Time*, October 15, 1945, p. 24 (unsigned).

first words of our death-sentence; and prove ourselves once more, hopelessly inadequate morally, and so in every other way, to survive the atomic bomb. Of course we and/or others would be inadequate for that survival anyhow; but in that case there is everything to be said for dying as near in a state of grace as possible. The job really excites me, and really seems hopeful of some good result; but it's terribly complicated in research and hard to figure how to reduce to a properly factual, yet properly generalized few hundred words.

I also hope I may write about the victory parade of the Chinese, which took place today, on the anniversary of the Marco Polo Bridge incident, in as filthy weather as the Caribbean could give them. I missed the parade—knew it only through Mia, who saw it all, and felt both heartbroken and heart-lifted with love for that particular people. All 15,000 marched up the almost empty Avenue (5th); cross-town traffic wasn't even interrupted for them; the women were obliterated in rain-things; the men wore uniforms and nothing else against the rain; their two large beautiful paper dragons were soaked and torn to pieces within the first few minutes. They kept perfect order against the mass of rain and the traffic lights, timing against the latter so beautifully that no unit was ever divided by the interrupting lights or the traffic. Along the sidewalks people were tremendously sympathetic, standing two or three deep whenever the rain abated, breaking up and moving on for shelter, barring a few grim die-hards, whenever the drenching became unbearable. If I feel a sense of being in love with any people as a people, it is the Chinese, with Negroes and Italians a close second or sometimes not second at all. On a sense of dislike of a people as a whole, I am far more uneasy, but sometimes feel it for Americans, Irishmen, Poles, Germans, probably in that order.

I must quit—very tired. My love to you always, and to Mrs. Flye.

Jim

By the way, I saw General Wainwright in his parade here—from behind, and 29 floors up. Even at that distance it was a good sight. The whole city has a kind of love-feast warmth of thousands of great and small homecomings; this keeps up by the day and week. It is lovely. And God, what most of the home-comers and those they come home to, are in for!

[New York City]
[November 19, 1945]
Pharmacist Day
(and may all your woes be little ones.)

Dear Father:

Thank you for your letters, especially the last, written, I gathered, in a gregarious state of mind. I too feel gregarious (for identical reasons) but (for the same reasons) not too bright. Still I would like to say hello and send my love. My hopes of writing this fall and winter are not falling entirely flat, but they are leaning pretty steep. I've done just a draft of a story which might with enough work be good, about the atomic bomb. But in three weeks I haven't come back to it. I've started a short novel* about adolescence in the 1920's—a fairly good start. But in ten days I haven't come back to it. And by now it looks too flimsy. With so little time from work and so very little time left for anything faintly recognizable as civilization, it seems rather too obligatory to work only on the best things possible. But those are even

*The Morning Watch (Houghton Mifflin, 1951).

harder to hold to—for anyone of my weak will. I started a book about the atomic bomb—so far as an amateur could see the consequences—but I haven't been back to that for at least 6 weeks. If I don't soon manage either much better self-discipline or the chance to do my work at least 3 days a week, I ought to go crazy but probably won't. It seems possible to "adjust" to anything short of atomic liquefaction, and I'll probably keep right on adjusting.

Supposing 2 to 25 years to go, what is worth doing and what is worth writing? Doing: if I am standing under a falling rock and see it, I step out of the way if I am in my right mind. So: as soon as possible I get out of big cities and any near radius of big cities. But from there on, what? At the end of the next war we either survive or don't survive almost total annihilation (i.e. of everyone, everywhere) or: we survive either as "victors" or vanquished under a world tyranny. Even if the annihilation is really total, I presume there will be gestures towards a tyranny, likely successful. But more likely one great power will survive nearly untouched. In that case all good and consciousness on either side will be equally defeated and will have equal responsibilities. What are they? I imagine things will be such that the maximum responsibility and hope will be to survive, and to preserve as well as possible the integrity of one's consciousness. Enter the problems, which is the more important, survival or integrity? (for they will be at each other's throat, far more than now.) I know nothing about any of this, but in some respects this seems the only thing much worth writing or thinking about. But that, too, I object to, for integrity means wholeness as well as intactness; in that sense perhaps the obligation is to act as if the house weren't on fire; to use one's consciousness as broadly and leisurely as if this were a time of peace (as indeed it is, or should be, in each individual mind and soul.) So you try to think and live casually and with pleasure and general curiosity, as often as tragically and as befits the circumstances. As for averting the next war, I see no use even to try. Everything should be rather preparations for the aftermath, if any.

Well, I must stop. Much love to you and to Mrs. Flye.

Rufus

[New York City]
27 November —'45
c. 2 a.m.

Dear Father:

Only a short note, to thank you a great deal for your letter, and for thinking of me on my birthday. This is also half drunk, and probably not too legible (I'm writing each word like walking on ice in tennis shoes) so regard each unreadable bit as the Smile of the Mona Lisa whose main significance is easily explained: more whiskey, please. So I am now 36. For days I have had premonitions: more solemn than any in years. Now I am tight, very regretful, slightly ashamed, as if I had turned up in that condition to watch by my own deathbed. A very strong sense of death. God be merciful. And God best knows what that may mean. But I personally hope He means that in so far as possible I shall grow up and use as good abilities as I have as best I can; and that neither I nor anyone I love—and anyone else, if I could prevent it —will die in any needless kind of pain. There are premonitions I superstitiously fear to write, but will: 1) I will die during this year, unexpectedly (parallel to my father's death at just that age); 2) I will be killed after long torture, by one or another kind of enemy, probably Stalinists, a few years from now (common sense). This is cheap drunken talk; but also, sober too,

I mean it. I would give a great deal to talk to you—chiefly aside from these superstitious forebodings. Knowing each other many years, we don't often either say it or ever need to; yet occasionally, and now, it is a kind of luxury to say and realize how much I love you, how grateful I am to you, how greatly I value your friendship. I have never known anyone, and never expect to, to whom Montaigne's wonderful essay on friendship could completely apply;—and wonder whether he did; but I never expect a relationship dearer to me, possible, than that I have nearly all my life had with you. I wish I could add to this the honor I feel towards you, so clearly that you could never doubt again, in any of the disappointments your life has known, how triumphant and great a life I feel yours is, and has always been.

My love to you always,

Jim

Thank you for your second letter. I fully appreciate (in every sense of the word) your wishes for "a reasonably good year."

Dear Father:
                    Monday evening, fairly late—
Too late for serious work, not late enough,
Quite yet, to lay the insomniac's nightly bait
For sleep, with cards, trash-reading, all such stuff
Beside which I, the crafty victim, wait
Hours, while sleep sniffs and snarls its mild rebuff—
I wonder whether I can manage better
To pass time than by writing a verse-letter.

I'll probably manage worse; but there's one stanza
Anyhow; and another on the way.
With help enough from lazy Sancho Panza,
Don Quixote may, somehow, get through the day.
Failing all else, that improvised cadenza
Lord Byron patented, wherewith to say
In bland disgression everything that came
Into his head, may sit in on the game.

For my main trouble, as I can foresee
Already, is and will be, even more,
That though I'd like this verse attempt to be
Expressive both of prophets and the law
(Maine's accent rhymes it) why, I lack the key
Even to unlock wit's and poetry's door.
Or briefly, though the impulse is O.K.,
I haven't, really, a damned thing to say.

The things most seriously on my mind—
Oh, war; free speech; my soul; atomic fission;
Whether the egg first saw the world behind
The chicken, or before; towards what perdition

* The only letters from 1946 were the following in verse. Actually, the first of these was written late in 1945 but never mailed; Jim gave it to me the next summer when we met in New York. I have included two of my own (in italics) not with any wish to intrude, but simply because Jim's subsequent letter refers to them.

Lapses all good and ill for humankind;
And other aspects moot to our condition—
Are much to hard to tackle at my best,
Far worse when all I'm trying to do is rest.

Then too, I've always felt that poetry,
Or even verse, if saying anything
(Not its essential business, but for me,
At present, easier anyhow than to sing),
Should say it tersely as the verb "to be,"
In language worthy of the kind of king
Kings seldom are, or ever were—to say
Nothing of most who take their place today.

But there, you see, in spite of these convictions,
Already, now, with several stanzas done,
They are composed wholly of derelictions
From sense and duty; why, they aren't even fun.
But patience! If my personal prediction's
Halfway correct, your best bet is to shun
What follows, even more sharply than what's past;
For heavy seas begin to hide the mast.

Well—to our muttons; which are jumping fences
Well out of earshot, if not out of sight.
This week, as you remember well, commences
My thirty-seventh year. I'm neither tight
Nor quite exactly sober. My defenses
Shaky and breached, yet hold. Eternal night
Enlarges to engulf my little world.
Soon, soon, my bugle bleats; my flag is furled.

All autumn long, through the magnificent slope
Of all the smoky year towards dissolution,
Much more than Nature—man's fate, and man's
    hope—
Have, in that avalanche, been in full collusion

Caught, shaped, and colored, ever, on a scope
Grand as man's very being; a diminution
As huge to witness, and as full of grief,
As if each star were but a falling leaf.

(Unsigned)

(1946)

Thursday, September 8, Dear Father,
(That's the first line,) if you'd rather,
Next time I will write in prose,
In the meantime, anything goes.
Even if it doesn't scan
I will rhyme it if I can;
Though my penciled emendations
Are guaranteed to try your patience,
I am bound to pull some boner
Working on a Smith-Corona . . .

Well, now what? So work begins.
Pedagogy barks its shins
Once more and yet again once more
(As Lord knows many time before)
On every gradus ad Parnassum;
Well we can't teach 'em, better pass 'em.
Let those eradicate who can
Man's inhumanity to man
Through teaching boys to kiss the Flag,
Keep their rooms tidy, kick a fag,
Follow the leader, mind the rules,
Blunt and ignore the only tools
That interest the half-mature
Enough to make some learning sure
If only people didn't refuse them
The right to feel the right to use them . . .
That which Authority thinks good
Turns into just that much dead wood:

And so perhaps it's just as well
They outlaw Heaven and in-law Hell.
That way, some fighting chance remains
For the boy with heart, and blood, and brains.

So much for that. Too much, in fact.
I'm rather weary of this act.
I really should abstain from rhyme
And so I will, until next time.
Much love to you and Mrs. Flye,
And pardon this abortive try—
What comes of acting on a whim,
You see.

                    Affectionately,

                                        Jim.

Dear Jim:
        You may be quite amazed
To get this note so strangely phrased.

As for your acting on the whim,
Much better thus plunge in and swim
Bearing in rhyme a message sprightly
Like Caesar, holding parchment lightly
As through the waters of the bay
He cut an unexpected way,
Than dally with the impulse still,
Letting "Why should I?" wait upon "I will."
Epistolary versifying
May frequently prove well worth trying,
As carried on by lines that scan
We comment on the race of man,
Moralize, question, let our thought
Draw in its net and see what's caught.
So, tight or sober, if you're feeling
The writing mood upon you stealing,

To it immediately give heed;
Obey the impulse and proceed . . .

Another academic year
Begins, now that September's here.
Youth, lovely, sanguine or unsure,
Daring or timid, warped or pure,
Veering between its hopes and fears,
Success, frustration, joy and tears,
Comes to be worked upon in schools
And meets far fewer minds than rules;
Learns much to be unlearned with pain
As crushed Truth tries to rise again.
"Hail! We who are about to die
Salute you," still is childhood's cry.

Regards to Mia as to you.
'tis always good to see you, too.
You were most kind to have me there
With welcome when I'd climb your stair
And hospitality's good cheer,
Whiskey and soda, wine, or beer.
Whether at home or in a bar
'twas good to meet and talk; there are
Few pleasures better than to drink
And talk with those who really think.
I'll hope for things of similar pattern
If next year I am in Manhattan.

At this point, then, I'll say goodbye.
From
        Yours as ever,
                    Father Flye.
        (I think that you will seldom see
        Such verse as this composed by me.)

Dear Father Flye:
        My gratitude.
Shy yet unshrinking, nice yet nude,
Transcends all bounds, except those set
(Broader than any fisher's net)
By pleasure and a new incentive—
Which, in so far as I'm inventive
I will, henceforth, try to pursue
Ad nauseam ad me ad you.
Yes, I'm amazed, yet it's not amazin';
Men's spirits rise to an occasion
As naturally as they slouch
If all the occasion says is "ouch".
If I can type you out some verse
You won't, by any chance, do worse.
And if you match me rhyme for rhyme
The chances are, of course, that I'm
Just damned if I'll reply in prose.
So much for that—and so it goes:
Much as we hate it, competition,
If friendly used, puts in condition
All sorts of latent faculties
(Better, I hope, than those or these
I sent, am sending, or shall send
Counting on you as a friend)
And even if it were not kind
Might stimulate both heart and mind.
Or, though *I* doubt Free Enterprise
Is good for us, or even wise,
I know that Freedom in the Mind
Is, actually, the only kind
Which designates us from the ants,
Or deals a fair hand against chance.
All that I mean is that exchange
Of stimulus, on all the range
Of feeling, thought, experience, need,
(As, humbly, herein, word and deed

Move co-abortive lockstep) gives
The guarantee that the soul lives.
Or, rather, that as you indite,
So, God help me, I will write:
No less, (and God forbid, no better)
Transmit the spirit to the letter
Than you; and you no less than me,
And neither better nor less than we:
And as for we, why, let me say
Neither better nor worse than they.
And so, elliptically as bees
My rhymes approach the clinching wheeze:
If we can do this, who cannot?
Or has the whole world gone to pot?
Frankly, I think it has, but here
(Although I grant you right to sneer)
I'm tempted to ease down to prose:
For all the feet and all the toes
Of scansion hardly can encompass
My sentiment without being pompous,
When I consider how the light
Is spent, which ought to burn pure white
In every man, and does so most,
(Whether by grace of Holy Ghost
Or not)—is spent, I say, when once
That light is carried by some dunce
Duly elected or appointed
(Or his by seizure), and anointed,
Who dares to say he represents
The People's Will, in any sense.
The People's Will? If they had any
None could impersonate the Many.
Nor, if that will were truly done,
Could Many deputate Some One . . .

Most that most people most desire
Is that the chestnuts in the fire

Be twitched out by somebody else
At minimum harm to their own pelts . . .

Most human beings want no more
Than they can see from the front door:
And that, intelligently applied,
Is quite as far, and quite as wide
As anyone has any need
To see, if he will pay this heed:
The world is made of just such views,
Little, not making any news,
Concerned, purely as you or I,
With all the immediate reasons why
It's foolishness to trust each other,
Yet suicide to harm your brother.
Almost no one wants war, of course;
Almost no one dares not use force
In some kind, every day he lives;
And almost no one freely gives
Anything that might cause him pain
Or even inconvenience. Gain
Hangs at our necks, squawking and wrangling
At best, and much more often, strangling:
Killing through all the flesh holds dear
All that within the soul is clear;
Halting, with force few can withstand
Each hobble toward the Promised Land . . .

Clearly, I'll grant, by any means yet tried
Most men, or all, are of their souls denied.
As clearly, a sick man in this condition
Requires at least a shift in his position . . .
It still is possible, I think
(Though caution causes me to shrink
From this part of the conversation)
To risk a major operation.
When everything is murder, sure,
There's nothing wrong with kill or cure.

So, looking through the shattered prism,
The one clear light is Socialism.

Here I'm afraid my logic fails.
Couplets like these ought to be nails
Each one hit cleanly on the head
And with one stroke sent straight to bed:
And well used, that's a better way
To make an idea have its say
Than prose, or even talk supplies:
Only it freezes into lies,
Half-truths, elisions and red-herrings
If, like an apple's spiraled parings,
One's thought, like mine, gets to the ground
Only by going round and round . . .

Democracy of vote alone
Is hardly livelier than bone.
Democracy that's economic
Alone, is not one bit less comic.
To own your life is hardly good
Unless you own your livelihood:
To own your livelihood's as bad
If, in exchange, your life is had.
To cry of your right hand, "I'm free!"
While your left hand, as all can see,
Is mouthed and mangled in the cogs,
Is not a freedom fit for dogs.
To sing of your left hand, "I'm safe"
While your right hand, like a street waif
Hides withered in your deepest pocket
Yanks safety from the very socket,
The freeman never can be free
Whose need misuses him and me:
Nor can the man be free of need
Whose self-respect must die or bleed.

                                        (Unsigned)

Dear Jim:

✼ ✼ ✼ ✼ ✼ ✼

I like your words on competition
Of friendly sort, not for position
O'er someone else to win or score
But as incentive to do more
Than if such challenge did not jog
And lift our spirits from the bog
Of sluggishness and petty day's routine
In which creative work is seldom seen.
(A slip into pentameters like this
May make a little variant not amiss.)
So thank you for the outside stimulation
Needed to spur a person in my station
To "take his pen in hand," and though he falter
Genuflect shyly toward the Muse's altar.

"All is not well," declared Saint Thomas More,
"Because all men are not good." And before
Brash theorists lightly undertake to prove
Some social nostrum's certain to remove
(Or pretty nearly so) our inequalities
And put our total population all at ease,
They would do well to see that More's words state
A fundamental social postulate.
(Not that 'twas More's discovery. The Church
Full well aware of human nature's smirch
And seeing it in Adam first begin
Labels it tersely as Original Sin.
Chesterton says Utopians oft are dumb,
Assuming major difficulties overcome
And thereupon proceeding to dispute
About some minor ones not worth a hoot.
Assuming men as scrupulously fair—
That no one will want more than just his share—
About this share's delivery they discuss
If it will be by train or motor-bus.)

So I much doubt that Socialism would be
A remedy for the ills that we can see.
And if for some of these it were some cure
Its regimen would be galling to endure.
What economic system would
Work well were "all men are not good"
I do not know (though some are better
Both in the spirit and the letter).
You take your choice of ills and gains:
No one all evil force restrains;
In any, some things are secured
That cause some ills to be endured.
Many a man should have had things that have missed
    him,
But much will go amiss in any system.
What Socialism would give I cannot say;
I know full well some things 'twould take away.
By its inherent nature it deprives
People of something precious in their lives:
The sense of freedom. They'd be regimented
And standardized. Would we be thus contented?
Some might like this, some not. I'd say at random
Simply De gustibus non est disputandum.

    •   •   •   •   •   •   •

Father Flye.

Dear Father:

In this rather short piece of spare time I started to rhyme a letter to you, and gave up. But I would like to get off a note, anyhow. . . .

I was very much interestetd in the equilibrium-of-nature data you sent me. What specially interests me is that man's capacity for intelligence and for compassion, though they are wild and unsettling cards in the deck, and appear "anti-natural," are also a part of nature which must seek and try to find their own equilibrium. One question is, whether it is sometimes most intelligent to go against intelligence, and most compassionate to deny compassion. It seems it is; but that, done deliberately, seems to me as deeply "against nature" as "against God." One kind of equilibrium is recklessness, which is in some ways akin to faith—i.e. in some contexts the only way to keep from falling down is to manage to run faster than the momentum of the beginning fall, as in running down a hill, or stairs, to keep from falling. I saw a movie this morning which would please you: a French film called *A Cage of Nightingales*; about a cruel little reform-school, not unlike an establishment we have at times talked of, in which a new man does wonders by using his heart, his head, his humor, and his ability to interest the boys in choral singing—and gets fired for breaking a regulation through which he saves a whole dormitory from death by fire. Some of what this teacher does, though often good in its way, you wouldn't, I think, like; most of what he does, you would; and the boys are wonderful. You would enjoy the rest of the faculty, too.

I do intend soon to find the questionnaire and send it—the trouble is it will require deep rummaging through a lot of desk-drawers and papers, for I have never yet worked out or kept to a filing system; I keep putting this off when there is anything else to do, as I keep putting off getting a haircut.

Almost springlike weather; I'm half-drowned with inertia. Now I'd better stop. I'll try again when I'm more competent. Love,

Jim

Dear Father:

Thank you very much for your letters and enclosures. I've been meaning and wanting to mail you a letter for a long time, and started one in the office a couple of weeks ago, but never got back to it. One trouble with our tries at verse is, I wanted to answer you in verse, on things enough worth talking about that verse statement of them would require more time than I had; at the same time I kept hoping for time enough, so didn't try to write a prose letter.

I think the main thing I wanted to answer on was socialism. I agree with nearly all you said about it, and quoted, except your conclusions. I can only be very brief now but here are a few of the main issues as I see them.

(1) In ratio to socialization there is loss of freedom. I see no escape from this but I feel there is a great difference between socialists who recognize it as a never soluble problem, and who would constantly work towards the best balance possible, always with as deep regard for freedom as for security—and those socialists who, instead, do not see this as a problem but who eagerly embrace and urge the loss of freedom, still more weirdly insist that the only true freedom is in "security."

(2) You say, and quote others as saying, that the

mere conception of socialism implies an inadequate recognition of the power of evil. I think this is true of most socialists, most liberals, and for that matter most people; but I don't think it inevitable or intrinsic. My conception of it—and that of quite a few others—is not fatuously optimistic, or even optimistic at all. I recognize its power, anyhow to a considerable degree; since I doubt that any individual ever wholly wins against evil, I am no such fool as to think that groups can. My conception of socialism is of something in which absolute victory is unthinkable; what one works for is the least disastrous and most honorable defeat available against great odds. Within those limited terms, and in that kind of humility, I greatly prefer hope and faith and one's best efforts, to despair and resignation.

(3) As I know you realize, I am capable of many doubts and qualifiers about democracy. But however great they are, I prefer it to any other conception of how people should try to live together.

But I haven't time to even skim these things now. One of the main things I mean, though, is that it seems to me morally and in every other way better that people would make their own mistakes than that they should live according to another's wisdom. Of course there is no government without force and prerogative; but the only members of the Elect I would thoroughly trust would be those who imposed their superiority, if at all, as lightly as possible and with the greatest reluctance and self-skepticism. That is characteristic of very few people among the Elect. (Of course I greatly abominate the common-man-sentimentalist who believes that whatever the people choose is for that reason right. It is far more likely to be wrong—especially when enough of the people believe that merely by being The People they are right; but at least this right-wrong mixture is a truer measure and image than any other, of the state of good and evil within that people as a body.)

I must stop. A happy Easter to you and to Mrs. Flye. My love,

Jim

Dear Father:

I'm very puzzled in realizing how long it is since I've written, to say nothing of being very sorry. I've thought of you very often, and every time, realized I haven't written, and every time have expected and intended to write the next chance I got. But I haven't done it. Not in attempted self-excuse, I am curious why, and realize several reasons. I've been very much pre-occupied for several months with a piece of writing I'm trying to do, that has so soaked up my interest that I've felt relatively little else to think or talk about. Added to this, I've been unable to do much of it except during my vacation last fall, but week after week has gone by in frustration compounded of my job, unexpected pieces of hard work for the job, the NATION, or in personal relationships, and besides, my own inertia, inefficiency and capacity for waste of time. This has gradually brought on an unusually deep and lasting depression, mental and physical, from which for several weeks now I've had only a few hours escape per week. In that kind of apathy I'm incapable of anything except, by desperate effort and will-power, doing my job. But any coherent talking is out of the question. Just now I seem to be on a tight rope between such depression and reasonable well-being, so I'm seizing the chance to write you at least a note to tell you I realize how long it is since

I've written, and why, so well as I understand it, and to wish you well and send my love.

I think I'd better not talk much about the piece of writing. A novel, short but longer than I had foreseen or thought best for it, about my first 6 years, ending the day of my father's burial.* I read you the little I had done of it. On the whole, I feel hopeful about it, and I certainly need to feel hopeful. Underlying the hopefulness is utter lack of confidence, apathy, panic and despair. And I'd better not dwell on that just now, either, for I could much too easily slip into it . . .

I find I am incapable of leisure without fear and guilt, and that seems a far from healthy state to be in.

There is a very beautiful French movie here now, which I hope will be around this summer for you to see. It is called *Farrabique*, the name of a farm in Southwestern France. It is without actors or a fictional story; it is simply a chronicle of a full year in the life of a farm family. It seems to me one of the finest things of any such kind—i.e. agricultural poetry—that I know. It hasn't the absolute mastery and beauty of the *Georgics*, but it doesn't by any means fall to pieces under the comparison.

Two very differing heroes of mine have died lately: Gandhi, and Sergei Eisenstein. Gandhi seems to me the best reason why this is not merely the horrible Dark Age it certainly is, but also one of wonderful accomplishment,—and conceivable hope for a future. Eisenstein is the perfect image of the Promethean type in this time. Well I can't write about them.

On about everything else, I guess, I'm overtaken with the realization that by Wednesday morning I'm due with as good a piece as I can write about Eisenstein for *The Nation*.** I must quit and try to do it.

God bless you.

* Ultimately, this became *A Death in the Family* (McDowell, Obolensky, 1957).
** See *Agee on Film*, Vol. I, p. 299.

But will you please tell me: are you in any way offended that I, who don't even know, most of the time, whether I believe in God, should say that? I realize my lack of right to, but I believe in obeying a thing which is spontaneous.

Will you tell me and, if you see any way to, "advise" me in general? I am often struck by how seldom I am concerned to try to clarify my belief or unbelief, but that doesn't seem to deepen my concern much.*

I very much hope that Mrs. Flye is better now. I have been meaning to write her, too, and I am ashamed not to have. Please give her my love; and my love to you.

Rufus.

* Because Jim raises the question, I have taken the liberty of quoting from my own reply of April 4th:
You asked if I feel it perhaps somewhat incongruous to have you use such an expression as "God bless you." I certainly do not. You are naturally religious. Some persons have a fundamental sense of reverence and of tenderness, basic qualities in religion, and of such are you. There is a quotation which I can't identify, something like
"We needs must love the highest when we see it."
I certainly don't believe that, as a generality. There are those who are bored by what is clean, sweet, beautiful, tender, reverent. As between the high and the low, they will choose the low. There were those who disapproved of Christ and those who laughed and jeered at Him as He hung on the cross. I know that you are of those who love the highest when they see it; *anima naturaliter Christiana,* as the old expression was. As between Christ and those against Him, there is no doubt to which side you are drawn. The way to make this allegiance open will I think become clearer to you.
With my love and constant thought,

Dear Father:

Thank you a lot for your letter. Yes, the experience,* in some ways, did give me "much to realize and
to think over." I wish however I could have thought
it over more. Many visitors, and a kind of inertia in
me, which kept driving me to read and, later, to try to
write (of entirely different things), prevented that.
The most striking thing was whatever it brought to
me of a sense of death. All this was highly ambiguous,
for I was unable to feel that it was at all likely that
I would die—hardly more likely, considering the
commonness of the operation and the skill, than by
walking around town during a time of the day traffic
is heavy. Yet it is a drastic thing to be put to sleep and
to have your body deeply opened, for the first time
(before, my total anesthesia has been for little things
like circumcision, adenoids, tonsils, or infected hand);
and late the night before it, in the hospital, I felt
grave about it. I am curious about what I did, and
didn't do, under those circumstances. I wrote Mia a
long letter, including messages to friends (and needless to say including you), and took care to leave it
where it would be found, in case I didn't come through
it. In writing it I couldn't either believe or disbelieve
in my death next morning. But by the time I finished it
I had written myself out of my sense that it was at
all likely, or even that it would happen at all. I then
thought a little of trying to get a priest to come, before
the operation; but could no longer take the possibility
of dying seriously enough. Then I looked out over
Lexington Avenue, without any particularly valetudi-
nary feeling, until I fell asleep. It did not occur to
me to pray, before I slept. In the morning, I felt so

* An appendectomy.

much better I was sure this immediate attack and infection were over. Since this was an inconvenient time of year to have the operation, I was eager to consult my doctor and, if he thought possible, postpone it. He gave me no chance to present my arguments—walked out quickly. A nurse came in and gave me an injection. I thought it was the routine "quieting" injection, which I'd heard is always given before wheeling you in; so I made no objection. My only further chance to talk with my doctor was bang in the operating room. I was blandly told that I was full of morphine, and so couldn't of course be taken seriously. It certainly weakened my capacity for argument. Besides, it was reasonable enough that the appendix should come out: all I resented was the railroading. So I submitted—and throughout my unconsciousness, apparently delivered myself of my entire complex on the subject of the pseudo-sacredness and power-mania of doctors and scientists. In short, I was too preoccupied with argument to think of praying.

All I can make out, then, is that I felt no fear of death, and no religious feeling. I would give a great deal to know how much more of both I might have felt if my sense of the possibility of death had been more acute—or if I had not worked it off, characteristically, with the thing that first concerned me: my relationship with other human beings.

Incidentally, I didn't have ether, but some intravenous anesthetic (in the crook of the elbow): no nausea, no dreams, nothing but a loose tongue; slept a couple of hours afterward; out very fast; pleasant experience.

No great pain from the wound: discomfort mainly from gas, coughing and laughter. Laughed very easily, the first few days. In fact, with loss of physical and nervous strength, and stamina for thought, etc., recovered much of my gaiety of about 20 years ago. I wish I could slip into that at will, and am going to try to learn more about it. I miss its wonderful pleasure.

I'm so happy that you'll be here this summer. So will I—until August, anyhow, and possibly then. I very much look forward to seeing you. . . . I am very grateful to you for what you wrote about the religious question I asked you. I certainly feel no doubt to which side I am drawn "as between Christ and those against Him." I *would* like to talk (or write) about your next sentence: "The way to make this allegiance open will I think become clear to you." In secular ways I feel open about it; but I mean more than that, and I think you are speaking of more than that. Will you tell me more about it? (I wish I *did* have a wire recorder; they're fine machines.)

My love to you always; my oldest and dearest friend—

Jim.

[New York City]
[January 26, 1949]
Wednesday night

Dear Father:

I've thought of you often but, as has always been too often so, without writing. Just a note now, for that matter.

Mother writes that Father Wright sees nobody any more,* except you, with occasional visits from Father Spencer. I'm glad you are seeing him. I think it means a great deal to both of them and will continue to, to my mother. . . . Certainly in essence they have always thought of you and Mrs. Flye as friends who went very far back and were very dear to them, and I think in this kind of time, that means more than any other people can.

It means it must be the last stretch, there. I hope so; I wish it were over. And I wish I could be there, for whatever small use I might be. I can't, until I'm free of this job for *Life*,** which goes incredibly slowly. The whole thing is sadder to me than there is any point in telling about.

I don't see God's providence or inscrutable mercy in such a thing. My intuition is that God is not a vulgarian. I don't think He so directs traffic that one truck miraculously stops short on a precipice and an-another demolishes a child. I think the former and the latter merely happened, and stand in humility before chance (with its conceivably traceable causes), not God. I would suppose that God leaves the Universe to its own devices (largely, anyhow), as He leaves human beings to theirs—largely. (It would be a poor sort of lover who obtained love by use of an aphrodisiac, or a cat-o'-nine-tails.) I don't doubt His omnipotence; but again I doubt that He uses it for

* Father Wright, Jim's stepfather, was dying of cancer.
** "Comedy's Greatest Era," *Life*, September 3, 1949. Reprinted in *Agee on Film*, Vol. I, p. 2.

parlor tricks, such as blessing one old man with cancer and a younger one with an ability to hypnotize the Master Race. I would presume that one aspect of Omnipotence is an ability to make laws for Oneself, and, having made them, to observe them. In other words, God is not a sentimental anarchist who decides to play poker when a bad hand at gin rummy has been dealt. He knows, sees, and cares what is happening; and the tests, the relationships of all of it to God, remain vivid and unfathomable; but He does not interfere with the Laws of Nature (which as their Creator He gave autonomy), or with the human laws of creation or self-destruction (ditto). In this sense I find that Mia believes much more deeply in God than I do. In her sense of it, either He is responsible for everything, or He does not exist. In my sense, either He delivers autonomy to all His creation and creatures and in compassion and ultimate confidence watches and awaits the result, or He is a second-rate God, a sort of celestial back-seat driver. In this large sense, she is essentially the Catholic, isn't she, and I am the essential Protestant? This is not a rhetorical question; I'm asking.

Another question: Do you think anyone ever, without outside help, knows his own vices or weaknesses? I don't. I thought mine was weakness of will. I think Mia struck much closer, with self-pity, which is certainly a great weakness of the will. I knew I had some self-pity; I even defend it, in moderation. But I didn't realize how much I have, and still don't sufficiently.

I'm becoming illegible and had better go to bed.

My love to you and to Mrs. Flye.

Jim.

Dear Father:

It has been a long time since I've written. Between protracted hard work, and fairly unbroken depression I simply haven't had the heart, or whatever it takes, to write, though I've often thought of you and wished to write or talk with you. I'm empty in the head of anything to write, now, for that matter, but at least I'm less depressed, and feel like writing, so, such as it is, I will.

The pieces for LIFE, I've had an incredibly hard and slow time on, and I'm not finished yet—but I think the worst is probably over, and that a few more weeks may get me free of it.

Meanwhile I've been doing or reading little of anything else of interest. Come to think of it, I did read seven or eight of Ibsen's plays, a while back which I had never read before. That's all the reading worth mentioning, which I can remember. Very lately I read Michaux' book on the Quest,* as I gather you have. I like the short squib sentences and sections, some of the observations, the calm subjectivity (the fact that he is at least as often pig-headed and perverse, as "objective", or trying to be right, or to "sell" you his idea), yet as a whole the book dissatisfies and even mildly irritates me. Too much is too ordinary, uninteresting or unconvincing. . . .

This has certainly been as bad an eight months for me as I can remember. I feel phases of something different from my ordinary depression and apathy: more like galloping melancholia. My confidence and hope are very low and at times non-existent. Yet in general I feel I just have to wait it out—and wait out, very likely, an even worse period when I am fully free to do the work I quit my job for—and that if I

* Henri Michaux, *A Barbarian in Asia* (New Directions, 1949).

manage to wait those bad stretches out, I will come through all right. But it scares me even to talk about it, so I am foolish to and will stop.

The way things look, I may begin to get free in about another month or so. If so, I will spend my time mainly up in the country. (Mia, having lost her vacation last year, thanks to me, gets both July and August this year, and unless catastrophe prevents, we will spend those months up there.) I feel exceedingly sorry about this, for I would so much like to be in town during your time here. But I feel reasonably sure I would work less well here than up there, and it is close to a matter of life and death to me now to write as well as I can, as soon as I can.

I'd better stop now and get to bed. My love always, to you and Mrs. Flye.

Jim

Dear Father Flye:

The books arrived and I am grateful for them. So far I'm just well into the Ruskin essay: I like it a lot and see in it a strong affinity to many things you feel and believe. I'm also very impressed and moved, by the engulfing sadness in his face as an old man. And for still further data on the horrors of Education, I recommend the notes in the back of the book—all the sadder because it is so clear that the editor really loved Ruskin and wanted to bring him to students— or to bring to students some of his own enthusiasm . . .

I've been so busy I haven't been down to the trial,* and probably won't go; following it in the papers and through the James Ball reports to *Time*, a batch of which I'll send along soon. So far it seems to go rather well.

I have just now a hand sore enough that I'll have to stop. (Just a table struck in rage over a piece of pseudo-scientific stupidity I heard of—I'll probably write you about it later on. No fracture, but bones bruised.) . . .

I want to thank you a great deal for your birthday letter. It was a deeply melancholy day for me: forty, of all things. I imagine that by fifty one is a little better able to accept it—by then it would be utterly impossible to retain any confusing delusions either of youthfulness, or of living forever. Now that the day itself is over, I feel neither here nor there, except that Time's a-wastin'.

I'd better stop for now. My love to you always and to Mrs. Flye.

Jim

* The trial of Alger Hiss, at which Whittaker Chambers, Jim's former confrere at *Time*, was a witness.

Dear Father:

I can't remember for sure whether I've told you that we were expecting a baby; she was born late Monday evening, May 15th. She and Mia are both very well. We haven't yet managed to decide on a name. They came home from the hospital yesterday. . . .

Not a good winter and spring, for me. I got a lot done last fall. Spent most of winter and spring on a *Life* piece,* turned it in not long ago, worked a week and finished a first draft, anyhow, of the story about Maundy Thursday.** Last week, work was of course less important than doing whatever I could for Mia and the general household; between now and leaving town I hope really to finish the story, and during the summer I have some hope of finishing the book. I've been wanting by the way to ask your help on a few points, some for the story, some for the book: What time, about, is just daylight, *Standard* Time, at St. Andrew's in early April (say April 1) and around April 12? And (as of Knoxville, there can't be much difference), what time is the beginning of dusk; sunset; full darkness on May 18? And what time is *sunrise* at St. Andrew's, April 1 and 12? And just sunlight, on May 18? Just roughly. Standard time in all cases.

Unless it's easy, don't think of writing. I'll see you soon. But if you can write I'll be glad to know even sooner; some accurate times adjustments needed in both stories before I type.

I hope Mrs. Flye continues well. My love to her and to you, as always,

Jim

A stupid note but I am a stupid guy these days.

* "Undirectable Director," *Life*, September 18, 1950. Reprinted in *Agee on Film*, Vol. I, p. 320.
** *The Morning Watch.*

Dear Father:

So Fall is beginning. Always the time of year I like best. I had imagined I'd stay up here and work alone till cold weather but it looks as if I won't. They are apt, I imagine, to want some work on the movie script,* on which I'd go out there; whether they do or not, Huston has invited me to go on a trip with him when he finishes his movie, in about 3 weeks, and if possible I want to get out somewhat sooner than that and see him work on it. In some ways it all fits together very well. I'm exhausted after writing and still more after typing the script, feel I could do very well with a breather before I get back to writing. So all I really regret and miss is the great good and pleasure of being mostly alone up here during these most beautiful months of the year. If I do go to the coast, and whether I do or not, I will expect to see you: for whether or not I go to California, I'm almost sure I will somehow go to Texas for a short while and see Irvine Upham. So that I do very much look forward to, the more so since I got to see you so little this summer. My feeling about living up here has changed; I realize it by how much I always hate to leave it for more than a day or two; to begin to be leaving over a whole season is already deeply sad and homesick. I just now look at an old letter of yours, from last Fall, and see the stamp, signalizing the final national encampment of the G.A.R. I have nothing to say about it but it moves me "historically" as nothing else has which I can remember. I imagine by the Centennial years, there won't be a one alive who was in it, barring some almost unthinkable freak—before whom, if I could find him, I'd feel like dropping on my knees. God bless them all, of both sides. It's the only war that doesn't just purely make me sick at my stomach.

* *The African Queen.* See *Agee on Film*, Vol. II, p. 151.

I'm so tired from the last few weeks work I haven't a brain in my head. No reading except the customary late-night trash: no music; few movies, and none worth mentioning. Mia had to take Teresa to town yesterday, to start "school" this morning. Another reason I feel the year, and all of existence so far as I'm concerned, is taking a deep turn under. She's been a lovely and happy child so far; and I've felt, however foolishly, always within my sight and reach. I know that from now on will be just as before, the usual mixture of good and terrible things and of utterly undiscernible things: but all I can feel is, God help her now. I begin to get just a faint sense of what heartbreak there must be in it even at the best, to see a child keep growing up.

Partisan Review has made a pamphlet of that "Symposium" on religion.* They sent me two copies and if you like I'll send you one; but I hardly imagine you'll want it? I evidently move, as I imagine many people do, in a rough not very predictable cycle, between feeling relatively uninvolved religiously and very much involved: though I'm not sure the "religiously" is the right word for it: but anyhow a strong sense of being open, aware, concerned, in the ways which are rooted usually in religion, or in the more serious kinds of poetry or music, or just in a sense of existence—i.e. a relatively very full and emotionally rich sense of it, as compared with the opposite side of the cycle. I'm evidently swinging into it again now. At times or moments I feel virtually sure that nothing short of coming back into a formal religion (probably the one I was brought up in) will be nearly enough for me: at others, just as sure I never will. But at all times I feel sure that my own shapeless personal religious sense, whatever that may be, is deepening

* *Religion and the Intellectuals*, p. 8 (PR Series No. 3, 1950). Reprinted from *Partisan Review*, February, 1950.

and increasing: even the swings away are less far away from it: keep some kind of relation with it. I wish I were with you and could talk about this, but even if I were I doubt there would actually be much to say about it: and though in a sense I like to speak of it (to you and, so far as I know, only to one other person, Mia), why in more of a sense it is perhaps still better not to—such as one is apt to say little about being in love. Essentially a very private matter and should be, and any expression of it is probably best indirect, if at all. Or "direct" in a highly formalized way. (I think for instance of much of Beethoven's music.) . . .

That was last night, now it is Thursday. I'll stop this and make some use of the masking-tape I got, to paint edges of doors, screens and windows, before winter. I hope Mrs. Flye continues to be well. My love to her always, and to you.

Jim

Dear Father:

Thank you a great deal for your letter. It meant still more than usual to get it because I was alone out here, over my birthday, and I take birthdays hard. Mainly a kind of melancholy about my life, a sort of personal Day of Atonement. And through the melancholy, a very deep sense of loneliness. So to hear from anyone I love, who loves me, is the best thing that can happen. . . .

I'll be staying out till middle or late January, working on a script with John Huston, *The African Queen*, from novel by C. S. Forester. If everything works out right, it could be a wonderful movie. If much works out wrong, it can be lousier than most. I think most likely it will wind up as good, maybe even very good, but not wonderful, or lousy. The work is a great deal of fun: treating it fundamentally as high comedy with deeply ribald undertones, and trying to blend extraordinary things—poetry, mysticism, realism, romance, tragedy, with the comedy. . . .

I haven't read a book, heard any music to speak of, or seen a movie or but one play, since I have been out here. For the present, I don't miss them either. I see a lot of people and like most of them. Compared with most of the intellectual literary acquaintances I avoid in New York (who are—wrongly—my image of New York) they are mostly very warmhearted, outgoing, kind, happy, and unpretentious—the nicest kind of company I can imagine, except at home with best friends. I have particularly been seeing a great deal of Chaplin and his wife. Very interesting, (to put it mildly) to see what a man of real genius—which I am convinced he has—is really like. Few if any mysteries or surprises about that. A very active, self-taught, interesting, likeable man: a blend or conflict in him of sensitiveness and tenderness with icy coldness, which sometimes disturbs me and would I think put you off. Perfectly unpretentious. The "genius" is a mixture of these things with tremendous self-discipline and technical mastery and hard work, with incandescent feeling and intuitiveness, when he is working. The roots are emotion and intuitiveness; the chief necessity is discipline. Well, I'm not getting a bit.

My love to you always,

Jim

[Santa Barbara, California]
Saturday January 20th [1951]

Dear Father:

. . .

Last Tuesday night I had the third of a series of attacks of pain (keen aching) in my chest, teeth, and forearms (first attack was the morning of the day before), and was taken to a hospital. By yesterday they had it thoroughly located and diagnosed—a coronary thrombosis—minor, but of course needing to be stopped from developing, and needing time to heal. That is expected to take about four weeks more, during which I must stay in bed in hospital and every way as quiet as possible. Then a few weeks convalescence etc., and then, if lucky, I will be "almost normal" again for quite a while, if I take great care.

This whole thing is brought on by too much alcohol and tobacco, too little sleep, too much emotional or nervous or other strain or anxiety, or even just too much excitement. The alcohol, tobacco and sleep I can and will see too. On the rest, I'll have to take my chances.

Starting to read France's *Penguin Island*. I imagine you've read it. What do you think of it? So far I like it, but with a little undertone of distaste for the professional skeptical ironist—or not really for him so much as for the archness he is so liable to slip into.

My love to you and to Mrs. Flye,

Jim

Dear Father:

I'll be leaving the hospital this coming Tuesday or Wednesday. Don't yet know where I'll be staying. Various very kind and generous offers of shelter, but I somehow don't want to plan ahead, involve myself, or tie myself down. For yours or Mother's possible convenience, until I know, I could be addressed c/o Paul Kohner, 9169 Sunset Boulevard, Los Angeles 46. (He is my agent for movie work.)

It has been fairly tedious but not as bad as I would have imagined so long in a hospital to be. Nice nurses, etc., without exception, and a couple of them so nice it is really sad to know I'll be seeing the last of them when I leave.

I still don't know whether I'll come home after a few weeks' convalescence, or stay out a couple or 3 months and earn back some of the money the sickness has cost me.

The weather is of course mostly incredible for midwinter, for anyone from any reasonable climate, but I feel stubborn about it; I prefer credible weather. . . .

My love to you—

Jim

Meaning Teresa Agee's birthday; she isn't really a saint but
she is much nicer company
than I can suppose most Saints
would be. She was here to see
me this morning. God bless
her.

Dear Father:

It was certainly good to hear from you. Yes, I would
ordinarily leave a forwarding address but for a long
time, where I was to be from week to week or even
almost day to day, was so uncertain and varying that
I asked the Beverly House to hold mail for me. Then I
thought I had collected the last of it which would
possibly arrive—wrong, as usual.

This hasn't been at all a severe attack; I'll presumably be out of the hospital by this Saturday or Sunday. But to have had to return to a hospital within so
few months and after so slight an occlusion as last
winter's, does begin to bear in on me. Just the
things you say of it—the possible difference between
40 more years to live, and 5, and that this in every
visible controllable way, anyhow, is up to me. I wish
I could take it a good deal more seriously, though.
Several things seem to prevent this. One is my continuing sense that if I smoke, for instance, really very
moderately, I'll get away with it. Another is the
whole habit of physical self-indulgence; the only degree of
asceticism or even moderation I've ever given a hoot
for, let alone tried briefly to practice, has been whatever might sharpen enjoyment. Another is an extreme
distaste for Absolutes and a disbelief in the existence
or necessity of most of them. Another is in some way
caring much too little whether I live or die. All these
things must at their root be closely related or perhaps

even identical; anyhow, all play into each other's hands. They set up a kind of blur or numbness in relation to every sharp imperative, and it isn't often that the fog clears to where I can see and feel and think sharp and hard (for instance): "All right. To use tobacco is for you plain suicide, so you're never going to use it again," I'm much nearer that today and yesterday than ever before, but I'm not there yet . . .

One way I can be fairly sure I'm in no serious condition is that I am so hellishly bored and restless here in the hospital after only 10 days. Before, in Santa Barbara, I stood 5 weeks' incarceration much better than I am standing this.

I don't know what the doctor would say, for me, about the diet you speak of: but I too am on one and am to continue on one: low calories (the 1200 minimal to health) and no cholesterol. So: no sugar, no cream, no milk except skim milk, which I loathe. No animal fats, high protein: so far as I make out by the hospital fare, something similar to your own Vitamin C diet is fed me as a matter of course. I get plenty of green vegetables. Yours sounds like a good diet—good for health and well-being, I mean, less so for enjoyment. (Friday: I've been meaning to add: I'm very glad it's making you feel better.) I have no talent and few tendencies as a gourmet, but I do care rather fiercely to enjoy what I eat. If, whenever I eat, I can have an adequate amount of some one thing I can really enjoy, I think I can willingly pass up a lot of foods I also enjoy (I've been doing so since last winter) and can gulp down, with each meal, certain foods I disenjoy, as if they were so much medicine—which is what they are. All fruits bore me sick, most salads, not all, leave me cold. I love cheese, which is high in Cholesterol. I like lean meat well enough to do without fat meat, which I also like. I like eggs all right but could do without them without regret, I think, the rest of my life. I like brown sugar better than white and should possibly use neither, and have never used much. I abominate "health" foods—such as shredded raw carrots or, indeed, raw carrots in any form. Between Fridays and the coast of Maine I've had enough sea-food to carry me well past the grave—yet I do like some of it quite a lot, if I don't have to eat it, and don't choose to oftener than every couple of weeks.

Wednesday night

Someone came in to see me: since, I've been so bored I could barely drag out from one half-hour to the next. I like to read and to write but I've been doing so much of both that they bore me too. Most of the time between then and now I've been reading Boswell's *London Journal*. Most likely you've read it. I love it. But after a while even that bores me. Things need to be broken up at least some, with people, or drinking, or playing the piano, or taking a walk—almost anything will do, so long as it is different enough from what you've been doing.

The *Journal* is so very good that it at once makes me want to keep one, and makes me want not to keep one which couldn't possibly have any such quality. I've always respected and envied you your regularity with yours. I've kept one off and on, years apart, never that I can remember for longer than 6 weeks or so, seldom longer than a couple of weeks. I haven't the slightest doubt of the interest of *anybody's* Journal—but I've been able to keep one only when for some reason or other I also felt either a great deal of pleasure or anyhow a good deal of excitement, painful or otherwise—plus some particular blend of faithfulness and energy which I nearly always lack. I was going to say I could only keep one when I am much interested in myself, and apparently that is true of me, and I'm not often much interested in myself (though, witness this letter, I yammer interminably in self-interest) (which is something not nearly so attractive); but it should be possible to keep a good or better journal through interest in others, and that I generally do have. I've spent probably 30 or 50 evenings talking alone most of the night with Chaplin, and he has talked very openly and intimately. The last thing I'd ever do is make an article of this; the only way it could ever belong on paper, if at all, is in a journal or in letters, the kind of thing which is never public until long after both people are dead. Both because he is the man he is and I so much respect him, and because he's also an intrinsically interesting man, I wish I had kept a record of all this. But all I've done of it is in a couple or three letters to Mia, and a good deal of it, though all of it interested me so much, I'm bound to have forgotten.

The clip you and David sent about deep-frozen sperm is certainly bleak. And yet if I didn't so loathe every trick of artificial insemination, and so much enjoy and respect good sex experience and I could see the results, I'd like to try it, and I'd be curious also to see the effects of it, tried out and checked on, on a sufficiently large scale. Like you I'm as much an hereditarian (if that word will do) as an environmentalist, and I'd be exceedingly curious to see controlled experiments on, say inseminating a 20th century American gentlewoman with the sperm of an 11th century French serf. Or to figure that you and I are among the last more-or-less libertarian humanists, to try that out and see where it got in the kind of frozen bee-life there will presumably be, if there's any, 200 years from now. That all may be controlled by "scientists," or "the state," or whatever the hell might control it, repels me very far more than in any way it attracts me; I very much more trust the blindness of nature; but there is a great deal in that blindness which is repellent, too. Begetting a child is at least as serious an act as murder. . . .

I too wish we could talk about a great many things, from the very personal through the very general. And I feel as you do, there is nothing, or any shading of anything, which I would not tell you or would for that matter, be glad and grateful that I could. Certainly on general matters I feel too stupid and inert (let alone ill-informed) to write with any intelligence; talking, where the exchange is quicker, and I'd get spark and support and opposition from you, I could do better with. I know a few things in general that I *feel* very strongly. I feel that this country is hitting somewhere along a new low, for it. I think it extremely unimportant who "wins" the next war; that everything they yell about as "Western Civilization" is pretty much over already and is being about as ill-served by this side as by the other; and that whichever side "wins," or whatever stalemate it winds up in, we're in for the same old Ice Age—which is already pretty far advanced, here as elsewhere. I felt divided on the British elections, I'd suspect that is about the last we'll see of any really deeply sincere effort to combine Socialism with the utmost possible respect for the individual; God knows it was drab, and sad, and more and more clearly and inevitably just another part of the glacier; yet I felt a real kind of respect for them and a sadness in its falling. But on the whole I am glad Churchill got in. He doesn't strike me as being by a hell of a lot the great man of the first order that some people scream he is, but he does quite possibly have some greatness about him, and even if he doesn't he's a *man*, which is more than can be said of poor Attlee and Cripps & Co. I can't imagine that anybody can do much any more, to postpone for long another world war or in any other way to appear to Save Civilization, but at least there will be some decisive and interesting action. I think maybe he should take charge of this country, too. There doesn't seem to be anyone here competent to. I think

I'm falling more more and more into caring much more for the quality or skill of the man than for anything to do with his politics or ideas—and to some extent into believing that forceful enough individuals *do* in some important degree change the shape of things.

I have a feeling I am being very dull. Anyhow I'm quite tired. I'll add to this tomorrow.

Friday

Well, I've covered a lot of paper but I haven't made any sort of sense.

Unless something goes sour I will go home tomorrow: further semi-hospitalization there, for how long I haven't been told yet.

Today (and yesterday, and the day before) I am quite depressed . . . I am depressed at being broke and unemployed with no job in sight unless—which will be my very last resort—I go back into *Time*. I am depressed that it is now over three years since I quit regular work in order, at last, to get down to serious business about my own writing—and at how very little of it I've got done. I am depressed because all the savings I had then have run out now (it would require several months of well-hard work by now even to pay off our debts and bills): so that the only prospects of doing work of my own, for a long time to come, are during periods of unwilling unemployment, such as now, and interstitially with hack work —which I proved to myself by several years' effort I can't do, anywhere near well enough. I am depressed because whether I am to live a very short time or relatively longer time depends (barring accident, disaster, and everything so delicately referred to as Acts of God—a pretty compliment to Him) depends on whether or not I can learn to be the kind of person I am not and have always detested; and because, knowing my own character pretty well, I know pretty well what my chances are, even though I will try.

And I am depressed because in another 3 weeks I will advance one more official notch into the forties, with so little done and so much wasted of irretrievable life, rather distinctly behind where I was, in most ways, when I turned 30, when, God knows, I felt things were going plenty bad enough. There are other things I *ought* to be depressed about, but I am not—the state of my immortal soul, for instance, or my mortal soul, for that matter. I think of it as a Laocoönic mess of some good and some very bad elements; presume God in any way I can conceive of Him to be considerably more magnanimous than I am (I would forgive another such trespasses and defects as I know in myself); and am seldom at all personally interested. If you converge these reasons for sadness all at once, the effect could be all but annihilating. It sometimes is. It isn't, this trip: just quietly sad and mildly sickening—like a tinny taste. I imagine, though, that my mental disease, if I have one or ever collapse into one, is melancholia—in which one is distinctly too liable to self-pity, naked or in any one of its ten thousand disguises. In one way I can't see why on earth one *shouldn't* pity oneself. Nearly everything I see or can conceive of is terribly pitiable: I can't suppose I'm an exception. However, I'd rather pity myself than be pitied by others—and, knowing the nasty uses to which pity can be put, think it may well be better to squirt it on oneself than on others. All the same there is something not just vitiating about it but definitely unclean—whether intrinsic, or through all but inevitable misuse, I don't know. It's the one thing that makes me weary about Stoicism (which in most other ways is so attractive—mainly because so aware of the truth; it is so often blended with, or a disguise for, self-pity—a sort of self-pity with its fly buttoned).

I've been reading a good deal of a book of dialogues collected under the title *Heavenly Discourse*, by a lawyer, Charles Erskine Scott Wood, who died a few years ago at the age of 92. Mostly they were written during the first world war; those which were ever published before they appeared in book form appeared in the old *Masses*—a much freer publication, I gather, than the *New Masses*, which I used to read and wrote a little for. I read a few of them in Harvard and threw them down disliking their clumsiness and over-simpleness. They're still clumsy and over-simple and repetitive too, but now I rather like them: the sentiments and ideas of something practically extinct —the old-fashioned, non-violent anarchist. Better than the dialogues themselves I like the man I infer from them—a warm, generous-hearted, compassionate, angry man who really *did* love freedom. I'm sure I would have liked to know him. (They're roughly modeled on dialogues of Lucian—God, Jesus, Theodore Roosevelt, Carrie Nation, Rabelais, Voltaire, Dr. Johnson, etc. in a kind of free-for-all talks on politics, sex-morals, censorship, theology, law, etc. A nice series on Billy Sunday.)

(Late Friday)

I'm feeling in better spirits now—thanks mainly, I think, to reading more Boswell. It's from his *Journal*, by the way, that I get the corroboration of my old suspicion that I'm melancholic; he had it bad, even in his early twenties.

My love to you and to Mrs. Flye,
Jim

Dear Father:

So good to hear from you, and I specially thank you for going up, later the same day, and finding about the Saints of November 7th. When Teresa was born, I saw her within 2 minutes after. She seemed to glare at me majestically, and I instantly thought of her name: Maria Teresa. Talking it over, we thought it too large and wide-open for her, but kept liking the name Teresa, intrinsically. Finally called her Julia Teresa. The Teresa divided 3 ways, about equally: the Austrian Maria Teresa, Saint Teresa of Avila, and our basic fondness for the name, with, as liabilities, the realization of the French St. Thérèse, a rather insipid or sticky little saint, and her probable diminutives—Terry, Tess, or the European Resi, all of which we dislike. Before we settled on this, I went into local Catholic stores and looked through calendars, the more thorough of which listed 3 of the Saints you wrote of, without, however, the nice things about the Northumbrian, (Bishop of Utrecht, I notice —and remember, from the Boswell Journal, that young Scot who studied law, went to the University of Utrecht).

During the hospital stay, and since, and probably from now on, I am on a non-fat, non-cholesterol diet. I feel, and look considerably lighter, and have not lost a pound since I last weighed, about 3 months ago. (Last weighed till today.) The main object is to get my weight down. However, it seems worth continuing, on my own guess, to avoid adding any fat or Cholesterol, even if I stay the same weight. I miss a few things—cream in coffee, drinkable milk, edible salad dressings and gravies, are the main ones. But it isn't generally hard. The prospects on smoking and drinking are harder. I keep the smoking down quite well. The drinking is much harder. Unless I can bring both down very narrow and continue in that, I must cut them out. Unless I can keep within a few quite strict rules, I am virtually promised very serious trouble within a year or two. If I hold them, I am virtually promised 10, 15, 20, or more years before any serious return of this trouble.

I get very bored and very restive. Many things contribute. I've by now read everything readable in the house, at least once. I've re-written and typed and sent off a story* without yet starting another. I am trying very hard, with mixed success, to live frugally, carefully, safely, etc. etc. . . . I know Mia is in a chronic kind of pain and sadness, in anxiety for me, because of my heart, and my insufficiently careful attention to it. I am out of work and out of money. The most visible and easy amelioration is through alcohol. It is something I must be moderate with, if even that. The only other possible amelioration or escape is through the hardest possible work . . .

To hell with this.

Good night. I'll try resuming tomorrow, and I hope it will go better.

Jim

Thursday 13 December

As so often before, I wrote an answer right away after hearing from you, but had hoped to add to it and so, never mailed it. After a few days of such delay, a letter smells, like a very dead fish, and easily gets lost, and is hard to think of mailing. This time I didn't lose it. It smells so dead-fishy to me I can't stand to read it and see, and for a change I'll mail it.

I guess nothing much has happened, since I wrote the above. The main thing to cheer me up has been getting a short quick job which I expect to finish in another few days: writing "narration," and paraphrasing dialogue, for a quite likeable movie, made in the

---

* "A Mother's Tale," *Harper's Bazaar*, July, 1952, p. 66.

Philippines, about the youth of Genghiz Khan. This will at least mean money enough to tide us over Christmas—or would, except for some ravenous debts. I sold the story to *Harper's Bazaar*, and with luck will get the check from that, in time to help out. I saw the doctor again today; I am back in pretty good shape now. During whatever time I can take from the job, I have great interest and pleasure in watching Chaplin make his new movie.* We may drive up to Santa Barbara this Saturday night to see a friend, Iris Tree, in a set of Mediaeval Christmas plays. Then again, we may not. I've been reading some of Andersen's Fairy Tales; by chance I knew only a few of the most famous when I was a child. I like them very much.

I've been thinking some about trying a story in the form of a long, anguished love-letter, in which the writer analyzes, pleads, vituperates, etc. etc., reviewing the entire course of a hopelessly unhappy relationship. The writer is God; the letter is written to the human race. At the end you might or might not remark that the letter was returned to the sender, stamped "Addressee Unknown." The basic idea I like: I think there are very good parallels about the necessity of free will if there is to be love, and, in that case, the inevitability of disappointment. But the method of treating it is, I'm afraid, too flashy and shallow.

My love to you and to Mrs. Flye this Christmas and always—

Jim

* *Limelight.*

Dear Father:

Thank you for your letter and for the enclosures. The review of course makes me feel very good—both in the simple pleasure of being praised, and, more gratifyingly, because he realizes so much more clearly than most people, what I was trying to do.

As so often happens when I get the time, quiet and privacy, which makes it possible to really write a letter, I am so listless and depressed in the aftermath of work, that I have nothing to say and no energy to say it with. So this is just a token note—a token of the fact that I am officially alive, and would be glad if we could be talking.

For the past 2 weeks I've been trying to choose one among several job possibilities: this has involved a good deal of reading, thinking, and writing. I think I am at last getting to a decision: a movie whose "hero", or central character, is a major storm; how it is born and grows; what it does to people, animals, crops and the face of the earth; how it is traced and predicted; and what people try to do to combat it or, rather, to endure it as intelligently as possible. I think this could be very good.

Thank you for the book on diet, which I have been reading with interest. So far the main effects I can notice, out of my diet, come of the absence of fat. My weight has dropped only a few pounds. My waistline is about 3 inches smaller. I get tighter, less pleasantly, on less alcohol than before. And I get tired quicker and more deeply and stay tired longer.

I wish I had a blacker pencil, that my pen hadn't exhausted its ink-cylinder, or that the typewriter was in order. I realize this will be hard to read.

I also wish I could get back East: I can't accumulate enough money to pay our way through a breathing-spell.

And I wish I could see you.

I mainly like Whittaker's opening article.* In a sense I even like what I don't particularly like, since it comes out of a degree of faithfulness to one's whole nature, which seems hardly to exist any more.

Sorry this is such a bleak, dull note. I'll hope to write in a better state of mind before long.

My love to you always,
Jim

[New York City]
Monday night, October 6 '52

Dear Father:

Thank you for your letter. This will probably be just a note, if that, to thank you, and to send you my best wishes and my love.

These scripts** *never* quite finish. I'm now working on revisions of commentary. Meanwhile they have gone to Kentucky and Illinois to shoot the film. If, or when, I finish this work, I am supposed to be there as a consultant. I'd better be, or this whole thing will be the work of New York rustics.

If, or when, I get that near you, I will find a means of seeing you, over a week-end. But just when or how, I don't know yet. I just hope it will work out.

I am now beginning to take seriously an effort to prolong my life as long as I, on the best of information, can hope to. Above all, tobacco and excessive drinking. So far, not seriously enough. I'm staying short of any severe drunkenness, and have brought cigarets down to about 8-9 a day, but especially on the latter, that is not good enough. And the pity of it is that alcohol, of itself relatively harmless, multi-

* Whittaker Chambers, "I Was the Witness," *Saturday Evening Post*, February 9, 1952.
** Television scripts on Lincoln, for the Ford Foundation.

plies by 5 my craving for tobacco, and by roughly the same ratio, lessens my power of resisting temptation. So I would guess that in order to get tobacco in control, (i.e., in my case, to eliminate it) I will have also to eliminate drinking; perhaps experimenting with drinking after the tobacco thing is finished—if it ever is.

Not an encouraging or even pretty picture, but at least I am concerned, trying again, and moderately aware that the issues are life and death—which is more than I've been in some time. So I thought you might be glad to know this.

I've been reading one of the works of Charles Williams, of whom you've probably heard. In case you haven't, he was a man whom T.S. Eliot liked and admired—a novelist-scholar-poet; one of very few contemporary religious writers who moves and interests me to read. This particular novel is *Descent into Hell*. He takes the supernatural for granted, rather than semidoubtfully or on trust, let alone in any shading of agnosticism or atheism; and has a wonderful gift for conveying, and dramatizing, the "borderline" states of mind or Being.

I am in general in a state useless to try to describe— as if "useless" meant anything: "suspended": heartsick about my effort in this job, its possibilities, its failures, both through myself and others and my difference in imposing what I know on others; ditto about my own unfinished and scarcely started writing and, as I feel, my nearly ended life; ditto in my living relationships. No desire to see friends, let alone make new ones; desperation when I'm alone, unless I have work to do . . .

End of letter. Tired and sorry. My love to you.

Jim

I hope you will re-consider, and cast your vote for the first grown man and civilized mind and literate

tongue to run for President within my knowledge . . .
Did you hear the Chicago speech, or read it? You
couldn't but approve, I think. This is quite a man, and
by no means a New Dealer. Immaterial, very near,
what Party he represents . . . Sure, I'd be glad if he
were the Republican candidate at *this* time; but you
can't have everything, and it's very seldom you *can*
try to have a man like this. I'm afraid he'll lose. Party,
etc. seems, in this case, of comparatively small importance. I am registering and voting for the first time
in my life. Wonder if it will be the last; or does that
become a habit?

New York City
[*January 1, 1953*]

Dear Father:

You know my remissness in writing letters as well
as anyone could (though for all that I'd like you also
to know that I write you probably four letters to one,
to anyone else), but at least I am beginning a new
year right; it is now 4.35 in the morning of its first
day, and these are the first words I've written.

Thank you particularly for your letter from the
monastery in Georgia. I take seriously and thankfully
your suggestion that sometime in the spring, we go
to the Trappists in Kentucky. But I won't even pre-
tend to contract for it: I've too often found that I was
mistaken, in things I had supposed I was sure
of—i.e. seeing you in the spring of 1951, and
last fall. Besides, in whatever limited free time I might
have, and above all might have with you, I think I
would rather see you—if it wasn't time enough to get
some work done in. On the other hand, as I wrote the
foregoing, I realized that there could hardly be
imagined so good a way of sharing time, and experience, with an old and dear friend, as the one you

suggest; also, that you are the only friend with whom I could share it; and now, further, that although for years now, off and on, I have thought with some real longing of going into some sort or degree of retreat, I might better and more likely really do it with a friend—with you—than alone. So I somewhat change my tone from the beginning of this paragraph: I think it is a fine and may be even an inspired idea, and I hope and in a degree pray, that we will do it. But to say "sure—first chance next spring", I have no business. I've been too often wrong before. When I finally got to Illinois, for instance, and found out the plane fare to Nashville, I knew I couldn't afford it; and since we worked 6 days a week, flying would have been the only way. I am exceedingly sorry, though, that I didn't write to tell you so. . . .

By an odd and very rough parallel, I am just now also much interested in a doctor-hypnotist named Erickson, at Wayne University—among other reasons, for this; he has, when it is needed, the mercy and common sense to go against the prevailing puritanical fanaticism of most modern Psychotherapists—the idea that the patient must *face everything*—must earn every ounce of his cure through suffering. With one desperate and precarious patient, he so worked that he a) cured her, and b) caused her to forget that she had ever been hypnotized, or even in need of help. This girl, at 23, vomited all over the man she loved, when he tried to kiss her. Then she collapsed into suicidal hysterical depression. He so cured her, in 3 hypnotic sessions, that she married the same man, and when last seen, two years later, with a child, was in fine shape.

The pencil is more and more blunt, and I have no knife and no other pencil. So, soon I will stop.

Monday I see a doctor I have heard much good of —a Dr. Arthur Sutherland—to consult about a thorough physical check-up. I'm glad to be doing this at last. I've intended to for months. No apparent urgent need, except an increasing and abnormal fatigue, or fatigability. But I think it needs doing.

I wish you a good new year, my beloved friend.

Jim

January 10

I'm in the hospital for a few days; nothing serious, just a check-up. Memorial Hospital at 68th St. and York Ave. But don't write there; I'll be out by Tuesday. I'll write from there, soon as I get the energy—about the Knox Version, etc.—

J.

[*New York City*]
Night of Feb 12 '53

Dear Father:

Owing you a letter has been burning a hole in my mind (but not on paper), for too long. So now I want to answer it regardless of any feeling of being competent to.

One thing that has kept me postponing has been the lack of a sense of time and stamina, occurring at once, to get into detail about the Knox translation of that passage in Ecclesiastes, as compared with the original. I can't try to get into detail now, but I'll try to say what I think in general. I remember that in general (not in reference to this passage) you were rather enthusiastic about the Knox translation; also that which you sent is one of your favorite passages, in the old version. The idea of a new version is surely as justifiable now as in the time when translations were being made out of Latin into the language of non-scholars; yet, (1) I don't much like what Knox has done and (2) I doubt anyone could satisfy me. This may be that my ear, and attitude are reactionary;

another quasi-mystical yet purely practical, even pragmatic reason may be, that though there is really very wide appetite, or interest, or demand, for an intelligible Bible, there may not be any sufficient depth of religious passion in either the demand or in those who try to fulfil it. In one way it may be irrelevant to speak of esthetic passion and talent, on either side; because one might like to suppose that if the demand were deeply felt enough religiously, between translation and reader, the esthetics would take care of themselves. I don't know how far that kind of inspiration carries esthetically (which is really, I suspect, the final or even only criterion). I know of things in earlier English versions which I prefer to the same in the King James; and of nothing of the little I know in late versions, which is within miles of either the King James or the old Book of Common Prayer. I've been told, and wish I could judge, that Luther's translation is even finer than the King James, esthetically as well as in humane-religious warmth and tactility. What I have read of the Douay Version seems deeply inferior to the King James; and there may be a point in favor of "inspiration" (the divine fulfilling of true need); for I would assume that the Douay must have been a relatively grudging task—an expediency rather than a burning need. Knox is better than that, in spirit and in letter, yet in all, he strikes me as essentially being a devout and learned and talented man of letters trying, with curiosity, and skill and a sense somewhat above that of expediency, to experiment with a task which would require "genius", or "divine Guidance", or both—which would certainly in either case require a sense of profound and desperate devotion and sense of the need. Taken of itself it is a good, even a beautiful piece of writing. But I find sadly few changes of word or phrase which make anything appreciably more intelligible (let alone more *interesting*, which must surely be at issue). And over and over again, substitutions and simplifications (and sometimes fancifications) of word and cadence for which I can see no reason except that he felt curious about whether everything could be done as well, or better, quite differently. Study both passages by cadence, as regardless of words as possible, and the old one is one of the greatest pieces of rhythm in the English language, and the new one is at best good, and never really bad. Start filling into the cadences the words, and the resonances, it still seems to me—or still more seems to me—that Knox loses out over and over. The best I can think of it is that to the occasional reader who cares to compare the two versions, the newer once in a while clarifies the older (a very right and useful thing, easily achieved by footnotes and glosses), and more consistently refreshes one's realization of the sublimity of the older version. All to the good: but the great new version of the Bible, if any, will reach not just persons of a certain religious-literary taste and curiosity, but all devout Christians who can read and hear English; and will be so good that the literary minority will have very little trouble, if any, accepting and revering it, and relegating the older version to the greatness which nevertheless henceforth becomes choked up between archaism and nostalgia. How much of course, my reactionary ear, and prejudices, may account for my reactions about this, I won't even try to guess right now. I know a good deal is bound to be highly subjective; but so far as I can know, a good deal is also objective; and I would risk, and like to see, the two passages subjected to people who are excellent judges of English prose but who have no religious background and—if they can have good judgment without it—no background in archaic English.

I feel slightly written out now. See if I can find something which involves less effort.

I learned in the hospital that I am in good general health, but that my liver is more of a hazard than my heart. The liver condition is not bad—slow on detoxication and on converting cholesterol into cholesterol esters, if you follow me (I don't)—and is regarded as reversible. To reverse it I am to drink a minimal 2 highballs per day, and must absorb huge quantities (you may be happy to hear) of brewers yeast, and of various vitamins—mainly variants of B; about 4 times the normal dosage of vitamins . . .

After long and painful indecisiveness among several job alternatives, I have found two I like. First a short job (or should be) developing into full outline a movie story idea of mine for the people who made *The Quiet One*: simply, a story about love, the way it really happens. Then, a movie about Paul Gauguin, to be written here and made in France and Tahiti. This, (so far) I look forward to with a great deal of pleasure. Pleasure too that I can, if I want to, go to France and Tahiti. Since the trip won't involve more than 2 months, I think I want to.

The Lincoln T-V films (which ran to an aggregate 2½ hours) are to be cut and released in theatres at about an hour and a half. I am seeing the first rough cut tomorrow.

On the possibility of a few days in one of the Trappist monasteries I have to be vague. The job may come too much in the way of it; and though the idea deeply attracts me in the ways I have told you, I also feel quite shy of it, in ways I imagine you will understand. Most of the ways I feel shy of it are, of course, simply the reverse-coin of the reasons I am attracted. One of the ways is apart from those and may well seem (or for that matter be) shameful and absurd: I am by now much more deeply addicted to alcohol than at any time before, I can remember. Yes, I am supposed to drink 2 drinks a day at most, but I have yet to succeed in that, except maybe once every 3 or 4 days. The effects of sobriety are intoxicatingly rewarding; but that is beside the point. Unless I should have broken the addiction, or would have gotten into a degree of control which still seems unlikely, I am afraid that several days of abstinence would bring me to such a pitch of tension that my stay would be much less like the relative apprehension of all that might be good that I imagine, than hell on earth. But I may really have done better, within a few weeks; work you care to do, can do wonders for you which you can't do yourself. Will you, anyway, let me know when exactly your spring vacation falls? I realize by your reply to a previous letter that it would mean a great deal to you, and that you feel it might to me, and I know that myself: so I am sorrier than, apparently, I know how to convey, to feel so unsure about actually doing it, as I do.

In some way this is a lousy letter, a mouthful of sweet potato. I realize I've said virtually nothing about myself. Maybe that is a virtue in the Art of Letter-writing, but between friends it seems a vice, I have nothing good to say about myself . . .

My love to you,
Jim

Dear Father Flye:

Thank you very much for your note, which I got today, when I was on the verge of writing you.

I had been expecting that I *could* come down to Kentucky, and I was looking forward to it very much —and also I had begun to realize how much more slowly than I had hoped, I was developing a story whose general outlines I must finish before a new job begins; and how sharply imminent the new job is. So, I realize, I can't dare to take out even those few days. I now, though, very definitely look forward to spending some days in your company, at Gethsemane, on the first chance we can both coincide. I wish it could be now.

I have had so little touch with [T.S.] Eliot, and have so lost the little I had (in which he was very kind to me), that I doubt I will see him as he comes through New York. But I will be glad if, without undue effort, you will introduce yourself as an old friend of mine, and give him my warmest respects and regards, when he comes to Sewanee. I feel sure that you would like each other. I may add that in a controlled way, he likes to drink—and is a great pleasure to drink and talk with. I hope this meeting may occur and that you will both enjoy it, and I wish I could be there too. At present I am working on 3 jobs: cutting down the aggregate 2½ hours of the Lincoln films to approximately 1½, for theatre showing; working up a few minutes in which I will appear "versus" a scholar (Alan Nevins) on *Omnibus*, arguing in favor of using the Ann Rutledge legend (as a dramatist) and in favor of a general respect for legend; and developing for the Film Documents people, who made *The Quiet One*, a love story, the way it really happens. The latter has been worrying me as too painful and sad, but just now, thanks to the pleasure of a friend to whom

I read it, I feel very hopeful. But by March 15th at the latest, I must forsake all else to get to work on a screen play about Gauguin.*

Yes, my health is pretty good, and the Brewers Yeast and vitamins are a noticeable help; but the drinking is a real problem—and more so, than ever before. I begin to suspect that the only way out, anyhow till I learn much better self-control than I have now, is total abstinence; which as a prospect, is so threatening that I keep trying, instead, to cut down.

So: we shall see.

My love to you always—

Jim

[New York City]
Jan 5, '54

Dear Father:

Yes, I was away—out in California doing some last cuts on the Gauguin script—until very shortly before Christmas. Since then, work plus the strains and confusions of the holidays, plus the disarray of all normal places for letters, papers and writing, plus general exhaustion, kept me from writing you, and from sending back the enclosures. I should have done this immediately upon receipt, and I can only say how very sorry I am that I didn't, and hope that you can be sure of the genuineness of my regret and can accept the apology. I apparently just do not have it in me, no matter how easy a thing is made for me, as you made it, to be prompt about such a thing. I have written letters, badly owed, which are still lying around weeks later, which I have only to send—and again, today, I won't do it, harassed too much by the lateness of my start on a day's work. For that reason,

* Noa-Noa. See Agee on Film, Vol. II, p. 2.

too, I can't make this more than a note . . .

I'm working, this week, developing an outline of a story for a movie about musicians in Tanglewood, Mass. It could, I think, be good, and it will, I think, be made. Many other jobs, embryonic, or hanging fire: my own story, here: *The Naked and the Dead;* a movie about Heine; a television series about crime, to be made in Paris; a movie about George Washington; a movie of Kafka's *The Trial;* one about John Wilkes Booth; a short one about crime to be made in Hollywood—but, as always, things take forever to crystallize, and one can count for nothing.

I must stop, and get back to untangling the Tanglewood outline. . . .

My love to you always, and to Mrs. Flye, and my best wishes for both of you for the New Year—which of course can always be worse than the foregoing, but may quite as possibly be better.

Jim

Dear Father:

Thanks for your letters and for your good news: best of all, of course, what you say of feeling ten or even twenty years younger; and the things which evidently contribute to that: people you like; their warm and sincere pleasure in you; the pleasantness of the surroundings; and, I gather, a good deal of work of which, I suspect, a good deal is tangible, and feels convincingly useful, in ways you have had relatively little chance for in a long while.* I don't know of anything I could feel happier over, than to hear of these things . . .

I read a piece by Adlai Stevenson, in this week's *Look*, which restores my respect for him and interest in him, very high. I'd like to know what you think of it. I'm enclosing an interesting piece from the *New Yorker*, about the Mithraic temple in London, and more recent discoveries there.

After I finished this phase of the music story, I thought I'd have a couple of weeks free. I had planned to drive up into New England; to see a couple of friends around Boston and perhaps to go back to Exeter, where there are still several teachers I liked very much; and maybe to go to the Trappist monastery you told me of. This has all been knocked out: an Italian travel movie I worked on, about a year ago, had been interrupted by the sudden death of my employer; just now, it became necessary to finish the job. I'm getting more and more tired of this kind of

---

* One afternoon in February, 1954, Mrs. Flye died, of a heart attack. On getting the word, James Agee with David McDowell (whom also I had known since his boyhood years at St. Andrew's) came down from New York to be with me for those next few days. With the close of that school year my teaching and residence at St. Andrew's School came to an end. After summer duty at St. Luke's Chapel, New York, I went in October to be Assistant at a large parish, St. James', in Wichita, Kansas, where I remained for four years; finding there opportunity of rendering needed and useful service, and a warmth of friendliness never to be forgotten.

work and less and less interested; it isn't a bad kind of work, but I'm using much too little of what I would care most to, and meanwhile life is rapidly getting a great deal less long. But I don't see what I can do about it.

Since I feel rather tired and stupid, I'm going to stop now.

My love to you always,
Jim

[New York City]
Dec. 4, '54

Dear Father:

I am very thankful for your letter for my birthday. What you say in the several first lines of it expresses, more clearly than I am generally able to realize it, what I wish I could realize at all times about the obligations between being alive, and what—including life itself—is given one. I've been finding more and more constant awareness of death, and the shortness of time, and of time wasted. Also, these seem to grow "organically", rather than through any special effort or taking of thought, and that—except for the relative lack of effort—I am glad of. But of itself, it isn't by a great deal enough. Too much of the senses of wonder and of gratitude are lacking. And there are still only the beginnings of self-discipline I need, at least until I learn much better than I ever have, to regard much in myself as the enemy of all I most owe to God, and most want. I was reading yesterday in Gorki's memoirs about Andreyev, that he handles his talent the way an unskilful rider handles a superb horse—racing it, beating it, neglecting it, never caressing it, or feeding it carefully. If I could begin to apply this I could begin to do better: but only through two steps: 1) continual awareness: 2) continual effort to practice according to that awareness. When I see how seldom I am aware, and how little,—above all in practice—the awareness comes strongly through to me—I'm surprised I have gotten done even the little that I have.

I'm currently, in that direction, trying to take on two jobs at once. This feels dangerous to me: I'm not yet sure how it will work out, but I feel it's a good idea to try. One is going on with the Tanglewood story, trying to get to the heart of it; if I can't within a few more weeks, I will not take on the writing of the screenplay. . . The other is to write a scene in *Candide* which Lillian Hellman and Leonard Bernstein are turning into a musical play. I will write of Eldorado, the Earthly Paradise, and this scene should be entirely in verse, entirely sung, and most of it, probably, danced. I think of centering it around three events in court, in which "the people" bring before their mild, saintlike king, not pleas, but three events or statements of intention, for his hearing, and his blessing: the celebration of a birth; the intent for divorce and re-marriage; and the intent to die. The first is self-evident, as among people who need fear no evil, and only sorrow which is to be accepted in gratitude and reverence. The second: the husband, in the presence of the community and of his wife and her lover, declares that he yields her to her lover. Candide: "But don't you *love* her?" Husband: "How, otherwise, could I yield her up and wish her so well?" Candide (after trying to describe the agonies of jealousy): "Don't you *desire* her?" Husband: "How could a true man, or woman, desire one whose desire is for another?" The third: A very fine old man, surrounded by 4 generations of his magnificent family, appears before the king. The old man is a farmer: "I have loved God; and the poets; and my wives; and their children; and theirs; and I have loved the soil, and have dealt with it reverently. Now, I declare my wish to die." He briefly describes two main things: that he has, of late, after being ever more grateful for life, decade after decade, begun in every way to tire: to long for the unknown, whatever it may be; and to tire in his faculties. He can foresee an ever saddening decline, which he does not wish to inflict either on those who love him, or upon himself. And so: The king nods, and signals; a draught is brought; he sings an extempore farewell to his loved ones and to the world and to life, drinks, and dies quickly and without pain, surrounded by his family. Instantly a sublime and serene celebration of his death begins—all white, silver, gold, and peaceful joy. Candide is much moved and perplexed: "So, you all believe in a life after death?" The king gently shrugs: "It is one of the few questions on which we differ among ourselves." Candide: "But you adore God." King: "Indeed yes. Too deeply to enquire into matters He prefers to keep secret from us." Then, comfortingly and politely, "Surely you will understand: we trust His Will and His Wisdom. The old man has passed out of our hands, into God's. How can we be troubled for him?" Or even, "His Will is our Peace."

And at the end, when Candide decides to leave and return to Europe—I must back-track. Earlier in the scene, Candide asks about kings. Hereditary, he supposes. No, they are neither hereditary nor by election. It is, simply, that (as with the Dalai Lama) in every generation one child is born who is unmistakable to everyone as the new receptacle and mirror of Divinity; there is never any quarreling about it. "Would Candide like to see the next King?" He is shown him: the most beautiful imaginable child. Candide: "Before him, dear Sir, how can you keep your throne?" King: "Don't be deceived: he is only a child still. Here too, sorrow ripens, sex ripens, wisdom ripens; he and I will know, when we are ready, won't we?" he asks the child. The child nods and smiles, and stands by the King's knee. Candide: "But—suppose he should die?"

King: "He won't: all others may, but not he. He has been struck by a fer-de-lance, he has been taken by a condor. He will live out his time." (Or other examples of the invulnerability of genius which approaches divinity.)

When Candide leaves, we begin with the ceremonial, farewell embrace with the King. Then in exchanges, songs of farewell between Candide and the King, and big choral blocks from the people. Finally, the Royal Child runs forward, weeping, and embraces Candide, saying or singing, "dear son." And Candide, after a deep sigh of wondering and reverent tenderness: "Our Father . . ." And all others, courteous and silent, glance towards each other: They have never heard of the prayer or the religion.

I am so much interested, and so glad, of all you write me about the people you have been seeing,—especially the two children.* I fully have the sense of miracle you speak of. I also suspect that you are an agent of the miraculous. I wouldn't mention this if I thought it would embarrass or disconcert you—let alone corrupt in you the power of which you may be the conductive. For one thing, no such imaginable miracle does more than postpone death, short or long. For another, if my rather wild conjecture of conceivability is right, you are well beyond vanity in it: you have simply an exceptional capacity for love, especially for the young, and through that, you may well be a particularly pure conductive metal for God's healing love. If this is so, or even if it isn't, I feel you are beyond any imaginable danger in having it mentioned as possible, by another. . . .

---

* One of the things I had begun at once in Wichita was daily hospital visiting, and I had written something about this to Jim. In a letter in November I had told of two children with leukemia. One, Terry Neukomm, a very winsome boy of seven, had had what seemed an almost miraculous recovery from cancer the previous spring. Now leukemia had developed, but I hoped that maybe this time, too, even if it meant a miracle, he might be saved. (He lived till March.) It is he who is referred to here and again in a later letter.

I hope you like the rough sketch of Eldorado. In some ways I think you won't, but on the whole I think you may. The scene should be a lyrical sketch of the best that is humanly conceivable and the keys to that, I am supposing to be: all physical needs are well enough supplied that gold, etc.—all our symbols of wealth—are used only for personal and religious decoration. The other parts of the key are: the absence of Theory; the careful use of Common Sense ("Reason") and of the Applied Sciences; Love and Consent among human beings; the Love of God, which expresses itself not in propitiation or begging prayer, but in thankfulness and adoration. (From Voltaire: there are no priests; we are all priests; and we praise and thank God in every moment of our lives.) They live in such wealth that their habit is a kind of rich frugality—of which the King is the model. Envy is virtually impossible: for every man can have what he wishes; he becomes gently laughable if he wishes too much, and envy is swallowed up in this tenderness towards eccentricity. I think of having an older European beachcomber, who describes it to Candide in terms of the seven deadly sins. Gluttony (for instance:) where liquors flow from half the fountains— (rose-water from the others)—everyone gets drunk, from time to time; but who could possibly become a drunkard? There are no laws, for the laws of love preclude that possibility, as Christianity precludes the possibility of a State. There are no prisons: what need of any, where the infinitely strong restraint is the despair one foresees, through causing injury or disadvantage to another?

I must quit.

I think I will tell you, my dearest friend; last night I had a dream, during which, in context of general dying (Mia was going to have to die) your wife and my beloved friend, as I arrived at St. Andrew's for her burial, stepped out of her coffin (without stepping back into life) and came towards me up a crowded aisle in the Chapel, and we embraced and kissed as we always have, after a long time apart,—as if it were only a few days since we had seen each other. She is among the Saints, and I think she always was.

Jim

Dear Father:

I will at least begin an answer, tonight, to your long and fine letter. Reading your letter has a feeling related to the epic—I'm not being facetious—in the building up of circumstantiality. I have a feeling that you are so busy, and so often interrupted, that you have tried here to write in a letter what you used to write in Journal form; that you don't have time to do justice to the journal, and find it easier to make a record in the form of Direct Address. If this turns out to work more easily for you, I shall be grateful if you continue it—always aware, though, of this weakness: to do it in this way needs, and deserves, full reply; and I will almost certainly be inadequate in that. All I can assure you is that I never feel inadequate in my personal reaction; only in my ability to get it onto paper.

I should say right now that I am very tired, and am only writing under heavy sedative. Well, I can't do other than sleep.

Since the Thursday before New Year's Day I have become vulnerable to frequent heart attacks. At best, I skip a day or two. At worst, they are very painful, and I have as many as 8 a day. At worst, however, they are still dissolved by nitroglycerin tablets, so that I am still hoping not to have to go to a hospital. I am of course seeing a doctor, and next week he will put me under special examinations, i.e. consultation with the best heart man in New York. Meanwhile, I am taking home-hospital care; with heavy sedation and 9-10-11 hours' sleep at night. It cuts down both my physical and mental energy, and so slows my capacity for work—and of course, too, for social life and for writing letters. Things appear to be improving: Wednesday was awful; Thursday brought one painful attack and two medium-severe; Friday, two which were medium; today, two which were mild.

I spent last Monday and Tuesday at Colonial Williamsburg, Virginia, the Rockefeller restoration; an explorative trip about a possible 30 minute movie. I was about equally impressed and depressed by the Restoration; as too Churchy, museum-like and dead— and was encouraged that when I spoke frankly of this, every member of the staff agreed with me. I like them very much; they are good scholars, and very amenable people, with a little of the sadness of faculty people (my age or younger) without a great enough subject to involve their best energies. The movie problem would be to bring some moment, some day, to life, some few years prior to the War of Independence. This particular problem fascinates me; for I have never seen it done, in films, for more than a few minutes, i.e. never done, out of any moment of the past. I am less fascinated by the purely historical or ideological aspects of the job; except that I can't see bringing the daily life to life, without bringing the conflicting current ideas to life. My general idea, in which they concur, is roughly: take an ordinary day, from before daylight until late at night, at some stage where there is "ferment," but not a boiling point. Avoid dramatizing any famous event. Equally, avoid centering on, perhaps even introducing, any famous men, such as Jefferson, Washington, Henry, Wythe, Mason. Try to find the moment when the several kinds of political antagonist, and ally, are just beginning to find out and define themselves and each other. Center it, for climax, on a tavern discussion, engaged in by some principal characters, merely overheard by others, in which those emerging, conflicting attitudes can be defined, and understood. Try also to find the stage, years prior to open break and violence, where the intensity of difference shall have the intensity, surprise, and honest pain, of a quarrel around a family dinner-table. Try so to use this little incident that each person, as seen coming towards, involved in, and leaving this dispute, and commenting on it afterward, has been illumined for us and changed within himself. (In one case changed in basic opinion; in another, changed only in becoming more deeply crystallized in basic opinion.)

As parts of all this—also warmly accepted by the people I would have to work with: two main things: the Loyalist or Tory point of view to be presented in the fullest weight and fairness. You may also present, as a Loyalist, a purely stuffy and acquisitive man; but if so, he is counterbalanced by a man of the highest intelligence and responsibility, who argues the King's Cause with the clearest sense, and who, by hindsight, in his ruin during and after the war, is seen as a dignified and even tragic figure. On the "revolutionary" side you also see some men of thorough intelligence and dignity: planters, who are too deeply established in a new continent to regard themselves as Englishmen or Colonials. Among these you may see one who is absorbed in the new French (formerly Roman) anti-monarchial ideas; and of him you show the pyramiding of slavery which has made him possible. Another independent is the vicious little opportunist-demagogue, who always lends impetus— and death—to every "movement." Another is simply the cautious tradesman; the prudent man who will always watch which way the cat jumps and join sides accordingly. And counterbalancing your intellectual

planter, a frontiersman: a man almost totally without
ideas, or any sense of opportunity, who by his own
independent hard labor in the wilderness has made
himself, all but unconsciously, a member of a new
race: he is essentially the father of Lincoln, and of the
19th century, and his sense of the changes and of the
land is essentially mystical. My sense is, anyhow,
that out of these rough ingredients it should be possible to make a kind of Virgilian poem, of a pre-natal
nation. And if I am right that this is possible, I would
love to do it. I'm not sure I want to take the job. It
would require as much work, for 30 minutes of film,
as two full-length ordinary films. But I wish I could
talk with you about it.

J.

It was good to get your letter yesterday. I haven't
much to say in reply. I'm a little too low on energy
just now; but I want to get this enclosed 2 or 3 weeks-
old letter moving at last . . .

To my great relief I last night finished drafting the
shooting script of the Tanglewood movie. Hard work
ahead, cleaning it up and getting the proportions
right,—but I feel the hardest work is over. Also it
now seems better to me than it had; so that from
here on with it I can work on relatively firm ground.
Part of the hell of it, up to now, was a feeling of no
such footing.

I don't think I'll try to add any more to this now—
My love to you always,
Jim

Dear Father:

As I believe you know either from my mother or from me, I've been put to bed for a while,—the last 3 weeks—and may have to stay there a while longer: a return of heart attacks, starting just before New Year's, and getting worse 3 weeks ago. During the last week these attacks have in general been less frequent and less severe, which doesn't of itself mean much, except for my physical and emotional morale; but it is also borne out by electrocardiograph, that the deterioration has at least been arrested. I will know more by the middle of next week, how much more immediate trouble or improvement I am to expect, and what that means in the way of inactivity, for a rough estimate of how long.

Until I know more, of course, all working plans are uncertain. I'm allowed to do a certain amount of work—which I mainly use to finish a job I'm late on: but I find that I don't have energy for much. Among the prospects, depending on what I turn out to be capable of, I might go to Ireland to work with Huston on Kipling's *The Man Who Would Be King:* or might write a film for Williamsburg (Colonial), of which I think I wrote you: or might, if I can afford to financially and physically, finish a novel; or might translate —or rather, re-translate—a play by Cocteau, *The Infernal Machine;* or again, might write a movie script about John Wilkes Booth; or one about Quakers during the Civil War; or might write another, adapting a novel called *The Way West,* a nice and modest, microcosmic story by A. B. Guthrie, about the main trends and forces in this country at the time of the migrations to Oregon and California. So I'm less at a loss for work than for choice and for time, and the question among them, of money, and of what I can afford to do for little or no money.

I've been better the past week, in general, than for the two weeks before—dropping, by and large, from an average 12-17 attacks per day, 6-8 of them mild, to an average 6-8, nearly all of them mild.

Not much else to report; this is mainly just to get a word to you. I guess the main thing is in reading the *Times Literary Supplement*, and the *New Statesman and Nation*, given me by Helen Levitt; the pleasure is that even when they do special pleading, the lack of shrillness leaves you your own mind, with a sense of courtesy intact between you and the writer, and the thing or person written about,—by *courtesy*, I mean also, a clear sense of mutual assumption that all three parties, however disagreeing, hold the fundamental standards of intelligence and humaneness in common. This will no longer often be found in the United States, as a matter of habit, in print. Might you be interested in either or both of these papers? If so, I'd love to have them sent you.

I'll stop now, feeling rather empty-headed and as if I should lie down. Rest of the night I'll try reading *The Infernal Machine* in English, first.

My love to you,
Jim.

Dear Father:

I hope and assume that not hearing from you means, simply, that you are much too busy to write: that it isn't caused, instead, by any kind of offense or disappointment, from me. In either case I beg you not to suppose this in any sense a reproof: the too busy, I understand only too well, and the possible offense, in time, would also clear up. I measure nothing by the frequency of your letters.

This is only a note to send you my love and to wish you, early from this end but late as you shall receive it, a happy Easter.

I've been better now, and up and around for about 10 days, with brief relapses. Unluckily, excepting Teresa, everyone else has been quite sick with variations on virus infections; these include Mia's mother, who is with us; and her step-father, who will be well enough to come down for Easter. This has turned the house into a Lazarette; to speak euphemistically; and has made it hard, or anyhow very unattractive, to work. At moments I wonder whether those who go, as I do, for a Full Life, don't get their exact reward, which is that The Full Life is full or crap . . . At other moments I realize equally well, that this is what Life is all about . . .

In any event, God bless you.

Jim

Tuesday after Easter.

It was awfully good to get your letter today; and I realized how silly of me it was to wonder about any other possible reason for not hearing from you, when I realize how hopelessly crowded with work you are. Thank you for the card you enclosed, and for the clipping about Terry. May God bless him and may he rest in peace. I can't write any more than this, just now; I'm extraordinarily low on both mental and physical energy. I'm enclosing a nice letter from Truesdale Brown (the Professor of Ancient History at U.C.L.A. whom you liked and who liked you), imagining that his sketch of English University night-life will give you pleasure as it did me.

[New York City]
[May 11, 1955]

Dear Father:

Thanks for your letter and the enclosures. Before I forget to, let me insert here: I just heard, too, from Truesdale Brown; a letter as disenchanted as the former was enchanted; he had heard some painful and, I am afraid, typical English snobbery towards an American scholar, Dr. John Finley, who was lecturing—Dr. Brown thought very well—on Pindar. So I quoted relevant parts of your letter, suggesting that this kind of snobbery, though exasperating, is small against the sense which you so well express, of the value of "the fellowship of educated men."

Nothing much to report. I feel, in general, as if I were dying: a terrible slowing-down, in all ways, above all in relation to work. I have taken weeks to do a job (about Williamsburg) which should have required a week, at the outside,—and through it, have missed a real bonanza, fixing a script in Hollywood, which should have paid me better than twice my ordinary movie salary. However, I am planning to retreat from money work, use this summer free, and finish my book.

The clip you send about dogs and cats is beyond comment: except my wish to be present, not with an

A.S.P.C.A. badge, but with a machine gun.* I'm a little dubious about my desire to kill, under such circumstance; but not enough to hesitate in talking. It connects with a movie idea I've recently had. At the beginning, elephants converge from all over Africa, towards a disembodied voice, the voice of God, which addresses them roughly as follows: "My beloved children: you know you are my chosen people. You know that—to you alone—I have given my secret: I do not regard myself as omnipotent. I gave that up when I gave to Man the Will to love me or to hate me, or merely to disregard me. So I can promise you nothing. What little I can tell you is neither encouraging nor discouraging. Your kind is used already for work; and the men who use you are neither markedly improved nor disimproved by contact with you. Nor have you been improved, or disimproved in that process. But now, a new age begins. Soon, now, you will be taken to be *looked upon*, to be regarded as strange and as wonderful and—forgive me, my dear ones—as funny. As I said, I am not omnipotent; I can't even prophesy: I ask only this: be your own good selves, always faithfully, always in knowledge of my love and regard, and through so being, you may convert those heathen, those barbarians, where all else has failed."

During this admonition, and blessing, the oldest elephant sadly leaves the assembly, and walks away to the great, secret, elephant cemetery, and dies there.

Soon after, men come among the elephants, and capture them for circuses.

We move, then, from fiction to fact.

* Writing him early in May, I had enclosed without comment a clipping containing a letter to a newspaper in which the writer told how a group of men who owned racing dogs had been gathering on the outskirts of the city for practice running. They would collect cats (under the pretext of finding good homes for them) and take them out to be chased by the ravenous dogs who would tear them to pieces and devour them. I knew what Jim's feeling would be, as mine was; and he expressed it.

This is what happened; a matter of record; when elephants were brought among civilized men:

1824: The first American circus elephant.

She was bought by a man whose headquarters was at Somers, N. Y. She was called *Old Bet*. She was exhibited locally. In a small town in Western Connecticut, religious people decided that she was the re-incarnation of Behemoth, and shot her dead. She was buried at Somers. A statue was raised above her grave. Ever since, it has been a shrine for circus people.

Late 19th Century: Jumbo.

The most famous and beloved of elephants, he died as follows:

He was led across the railroad yards to his private car. A gap was left, in a long line of freight cars, for his crossing. But for this gap, the tracks were hemmed in by linked cars. This was at night. No train was scheduled. But an express came through. Jumbo, seeing it, remembered the gap and turned and ran for it. He ran so hard he overshot it. He turned again, and met the locomotive head-on. He was instantly killed; the locomotive was derailed.

1916: Tennessee: Mary.

In a small Tennessee town—out of what charming provocations you can imagine—Mary went berserk, and killed three men. The general populace decided, accordingly, that she should be hanged. They strung her up to a railroad derrick; she broke it down by sheer weight. They got a stronger derrick: after two hours, Mary died, hanged by the neck, while 5,000 oafs looked on.

1934: Grand Finale.

The greatest choreographer of his time, George Balanchine, instructs the greatest elephant corps of any time, in ballet. The elephants are embarrassed, but dutiful. The big night comes. They dance to music by Stravinsky, in pink tutus. They do very nicely;

hardly a mistake. But all through the performance, people roar with joy at their clumsiness, and their dutifulness. The elephants are deeply shamed. Later that night the wisest of them, extending his trunk, licks up a dying cigar-butt, and drops it in fresh straw. All 36 elephants die in the fire. Their huge souls, light as clouds, settle like doves, in the great secret cemetery back in Africa—

And perhaps God speaks, tenderly, again; perhaps saying: "The Peace of God, which passeth all understanding . . ." etc.

Almost nobody I've described it to likes this idea, except me. It has its weaknesses, but I like it. I hope you do.

I must stop for now. My love to you—

Jim*

* This last letter was never posted. In an Air Mail envelope, stamped and addressed, it was placed as outgoing mail on the mantel in the living room of his house, where I later found it.

* * * *

Toward sunset in Wichita, Monday, May 16, 1955, there was a telephone call for me from New York. It was pleasant to be greeted by the voice of a friend, David McDowell—and then I heard four words, "Jim died this afternoon."

I took the night plane, and in the dawn of a May morning was in New York.

Thursday, at ten o'clock, in St. Luke's Chapel, not very far from where he had lived, we held his funeral: the Burial Office and a simple Requiem; after which a little group of us—the immediate family and just a few others—drove up to his place in the country a few miles from Hillsdale which he had loved so much; and there, on a knoll looking out over the wooded valley and the hills beyond, a place of great peace, we committed his body to the earth, with the words from that Book of Common Prayer whose pure English he loved, "In sure and certain hope . . ."

CHRONOLOGY OF REFERENCES
IN THE LETTERS

1936—Summer	—spent eight weeks with Walker Evans in Alabama, interviewing and photographing tenant families for a series of *Fortune* articles.
1939—	—married to Alma Mailman.
	—began reviewing books for *Time*.
1940—March 20	—birth of Joel Agee, his first son.
1941—Autumn	—*Let Us Now Praise Famous Men* published by Houghton Mifflin.
	—began reviewing films for *Time*.
1942—December 26 to September 4, 1948	—wrote a signed column on films for *The Nation*.
1945—Autumn	—began writing special feature stories for *Time*.
1946—	—married to Mia Fritsch.
—November 7	—birth of Julia Teresa Agee, his first daughter.
1948—	—commentary for Helen Levitt's film *The Quiet One*.
	—left *Time*, and under contract to Huntington Hartford, wrote film scripts based on two Stephen Crane stories, *The Blue Hotel* and *The Bride Comes to Yellow Sky*.
1949—September 3	—"Comedy's Greatest Era," a study of silent film comedians, published in *Life*.
1950—May 15	—birth of Andrea Maria Agee, his second daughter.
—September 18	—"Undirectable Director," a portrait of John Huston, published in *Life*.
—Autumn	—to California, to work with Huston on a script of *The African Queen*, based on C. S. Forester's novel.
1951—April	—*The Morning Watch* published by Houghton Mifflin.

1952—	—wrote script for a life of Lincoln, commissioned by the Ford Foundation especially for television.
—July	—"A Mother's Tale" published in *Harper's Bazaar*.
1953—	—wrote script for *Noa-Noa*, based on Paul Gauguin's diary.
1954—	—wrote script for *The Night of the Hunter*, based on a novel by Davis Grubb.
—September 6	—birth of John Alexander Agee, his second son.
1955—May 16	—death by heart attack while riding in a taxicab in New York City.